THE ACT OF CHANGE MANAGEMENT

THE ACT OF CHANGE MANAGEMENT
A PRINCIPLED APPROACH FOR LEADERS

Steve Mathew

iUniverse, Inc.
Bloomington

THE ACT OF CHANGE MANAGEMENT
A PRINCIPLED APPROACH FOR LEADERS

Copyright © 2011 by Steve Mathew.

All rights reserved. No part of this book may be used or reproduced by any means, graphic, electronic, or mechanical, including photocopying, recording, taping or by any information storage retrieval system without the written permission of the publisher except in the case of brief quotations embodied in critical articles and reviews.

iUniverse books may be ordered through booksellers or by contacting:

iUniverse
1663 Liberty Drive
Bloomington, IN 47403
www.iuniverse.com
1-800-Authors (1-800-288-4677)

Because of the dynamic nature of the Internet, any web addresses or links contained in this book may have changed since publication and may no longer be valid. The views expressed in this work are solely those of the author and do not necessarily reflect the views of the publisher, and the publisher hereby disclaims any responsibility for them.

Any people depicted in stock imagery provided by Thinkstock are models, and such images are being used for illustrative purposes only.
Certain stock imagery © Thinkstock.

ISBN: 978-1-4620-5073-4 (sc)
ISBN: 978-1-4620-5074-1 (ebk)

Printed in the United States of America

iUniverse rev. date: 09/06/2011

TABLE OF CONTENTS

Introduction to the Change Journey xiii

Chapter 1   Vision & Dynamics of Change 1

- o   Hyper Sight 2
- o   Principles & Values 3
- o   Living The Change 4
- o   Thinking Big Working Small 4
- o   Creating The Ideal Picture 6
- o   Where To Focus Change 9
- o   Why Change At All? 11
- o   The Change Leader Role 12
- o   Change Is An Unpopular Concept 12
- o   Lack Of Resources 14
- o   Building Momentum 15
- o   Perception Of Loss & Discomfort 15
- o   Review Of Key Principles 18

Chapter 2   Change Models & ACT 20

- o   Pareto & People Investment 21
- o   Kotter & "Operationalizing Change" 22
- o   Leadership Credibility: Kouzes & Posner 23
- o   Gladwell & 20% Critical Mass 23
- o   The ACT Model Of Change Management 26
- o   The Introspective Leader 27
- o   The Authentic Leader 27
- o   Teachable Moments 28
- o   Check-Ins 30
- o   The Power Of Proximity 32
- o   ACT In Contrast To Other Change Models 34
- o   Review Of Key Principles 35

Chapter 3   Integrate ACT Into You, As The Change Leader 36

- o   Integrity 36
- o   Assertiveness 37
- o   Assertive Language and Words 39
- o   Assertive Body Language 40
- o   Assertiveness In Situations & Environment 42
- o   Collaboration 43
- o   Transparency 45
- o   Fundamental Attribution Bias 47
- o   ACT Expanded Beyond The Workplace 48
- o   Persevering Through Adversity 48
- o   Transcendence 49
- o   ACT & The Change Continuum 52

Chapter 4   Employee Achievement & Aptitude 56

- o   Change Agent 58
- o   Status Quo 59
- o   Instigator 61
- o   Burnouts 62
- o   Assessing Attitude & Achievement Using 80/20 & Critical Mass 64
- o   Worksheet #1 64
- o   Worksheet #2 65
- o   Graphing Analysis 66
- o   Traditional Thinking 72
- o   Changing Mindset 73

Chapter 5   Assessing Organizational Culture & Influencing Behavior Change 75

- o   Workplace Culture Assessment 75
- o   The Significance Of Workplace Culture 78
- o   Strategic Recruiting 79
- o   High Risk High Reward 81
- o   Entitlement Culture 81
- o   Achievement Culture 81

The ACT of Change Management

- Family Versus Team 82
- Bridging The Gap 83
- Shaking Up The Culture 83
- Persuasion To Change 87
- "Tipping" Towards Change 89

Chapter 6   The ACT of Empowerment 93

- The ACT Of "Dis-empowerment?" 93
- Traditional Hierarchical Structure 96
- Selfless Leadership 97
- Your Blind Spot 98
- Johari Window 100
- Multiple Source Feedback 102
- The Coaching Relationship 104
- COACHING Relationship - SELF Assessment 105
- Parallel Process Of Coaching 108
- Ten Principles Of Effective Coaching 110

Chapter 7   The ACT of Recognition 115

- Recognition & Retention 117
- Herzberg's Motivation-Hygiene Theory 118
- Adams' Equity Theory 118
- Performance Appraisal: Investment 119
- Giving Feedback Using The Hamburger Method 120
- Reframing In The Positive 121
- Body Language 123
- Separating Issues 123
- Time Out/Homework 123
- Negotiation Theory 101 124
- Argument Perspective: Needs Versus Wants 125
- Putting It Together: Conflict Style & Argument Perspective 126
- Principles Of Financial Investment 129
- Formal & Informal Recognition 131
- Beware Of The "Template" 132

Chapter 8 The ACT of Performance Management 135

- Leadership As A Reflective Practice 136
- Not To Decide Is To Decide..............................137
- Quit Your Job 137
- In The Wrong Line Of Work 138
- Profiling The Problem Employee.....................138
- THE PROBLEM EMPLOYEE PROFILE 139
- Positive Spin: Can Problem Employees Be Useful?.......141
- Negative Employee As A Barometer 142
- Declaration Of War...143
- Psychopathology Of Negative Employees.....145
- Sun Tzu & The Art Of Performance Management 147
- Principles & Goals Of Performance Management 150

Chapter 9 Making the Case for ACT 157

- Case Study Organization A: Empowering The Change Agents 158
- Blitz Remediation: Mass Performance Management......163
- Case Study Organization B: Blitz Remediation 166

Chapter 10 Conclusion & Review of Key Principles..................171

- Whatever Became Of Nathan?.......................171
- Support: Above, Beside & Below 174
- Review Of Key Principles................................175

Bibliography..185

Index 189

About the Author 193

ACKNOWLEDGEMENTS

My good friends and business partners: Ellen Mackenzie and Michelle Donald.

My superiors, who have mentored and opened doors of opportunity throughout my career.

My colleagues and close friends, who supported me over the years.

To all of my staff, who I have had the privilege of working beside and who have made me better.

My clients, who have taught me that I am broken and need healing too.

My family, who have inspired me to be the best I can be.

Cover and graphic design:
Joanne Howard www.smalldogdesign.ca

Website:
www.mdmconsulting.ca

DEDICATED TO

My wife and best friend Denise Mathew, without whom none of this would have been possible.

INTRODUCTION TO THE CHANGE JOURNEY

<u>WARNING: BEFORE YOU READ THIS BOOK</u>

Participants who embark on the journey of change management will likely experience the following:

Budgetary shortfalls	Excessive meetings
Excessive work hours	Fear
Excessive workload	Anxiety/Depression
Increased labor management problems	Stress
Employees resistance	Sleep deprivation
Time management pressures	Self doubt
Excessive paperwork	

Some might ask why an author would begin a book with such a daunting introduction. They might ask themselves if there is any point in reading the rest of the book if the opening appears to be so bleak and depressing. The truth is that change leadership comes at a very high cost, in particular to the change leader themselves.

Over the years I have spent in various leadership roles, I have had the privilege of attending both seminars and workshops on management topics. I have also read numerous books by outstanding authors who are well credentialed in their fields and looked upon as business "gurus and experts." What I noticed was that, although their material was very thought provoking and well researched, the background of the authors themselves somehow distanced them from the reality of their audience or readers. Specifically, most of the "experts" writing the books or speaking at the seminars tended to do so from one of two perspectives: executive or academic.

The academics tended to be people with PhD's who did research and published articles or wrote books on their research. What was missing from their approach was an ability to connect with me, the front line manager. I would wonder if these speakers and authors could actually implement what they were proposing, as opposed to just talking about it on a theoretical level. I often walked away thinking, "that sounds nice—but it could not be used where I work."

Then there were the executive gurus. As a frontline leader, the question I often asked myself of them was whether or not they actually had experience managing at a frontline level. I also wondered if they had experience with the operational duties and responsibilities that constitute the everyday grind of most supervisors and managers. They talked about change at a Fortune 500 level, but I walked away wondering if they understood that sometimes it's those little operational things—tasks a frontline manager is faced with on a regular basis—that can makes a big difference down the road. Could the executive speakers and authors appreciate what it is like to manage in a hostile environment, such as a heavily unionized organization? Did they understand collective bargaining agreements, mediations, arbitrations? And do they understand the barriers to making positive changes those processes create?

To illustrate, I would like to introduce you to Nathan, who had just started as a front line manager in a hospital. It was his first week on the job and he attended a monthly management meeting, which consisted of all the frontline managers, directors and senior executives. As was the custom, any new managers were introduced to and welcomed by the rest of the group. Nathan was introduced by one of the directors: "please welcome Nathan, he is the new manager of the (blank) program." Suddenly from across the room, one of the senior directors stood up and heckled: "good luck with that." Instantly a chorus of laughter was heard across the room. Sadly, Nathan was the only one not in on the joke. What Nathan came to realize later was that he had inherited a program that held the record for the highest number of

The ACT of Change Management

labor management problems in the entire hospital. Ironically, that was not mentioned in his job interview. Nathan's experience illustrates challenges experienced during his change journey. Every successful change leader will no doubt experience similar challenges, including:

Budgetary Shortfalls

The cost of performance managing problem employees often results in increased absenteeism and replacement costs. The legal costs of mediations, arbitrations and settlements also took a toll on his budget.

Excessive Work Hours, Workload & Time Management Pressures

In addition to fulfilling regular operational duties, the change process often requires extra time for planning and dealing with the unanticipated crises that emerge as a result of the process. Despite the implementation of a change process, deadlines still have to be met, and that is on top of doing damage control.

Employee Resistance & Increased Labor Management Problems

The fear of change is a powerful motivator, often instigating negativity among frontline employees. The more a change leader advances an agenda and upsets the status quo, the more that leader draws attack.

Excessive Paperwork

Performance management is not an eco-friendly process when it comes to paperwork. Countless hours are spent note-taking, updating personnel files and investigation summaries and fact finding during the labor management process.

Excessive Meetings

The more problems a leadership team solves, the more problems emerge. Coordinating meetings with team members and stakeholders can be challenging, and getting the right people the right information at the right time is not always easy.

Fear, Anxiety, Depression, Stress & Self-Doubt

The subject of the psychological toll on change leaders is seldom written about or even acknowledged. Yet, leaders take their work home and challenges in the workplace affect a leader's entire being, including familial and interpersonal relationships. This needs to be acknowledged and dealt with head on.

Sleep Deprivation

The physiological toll goes hand and hand with the psychological toll. A leader who is wholly invested in their work does not simply turn off the mind after work hours.

As was the case with Nathan, the sad reality is that no one warns the front line change leader about any of these consequences that result from implementing change. In the seminars I attended and the books I read, I did not find any warnings about these issues. Instead, I discovered them the hard way. Thus, another motivation for writing this book was to prepare others for the cost of change on the leader and the price they might have to pay if they choose to take on that role.

This book was first a seminar. The reaction and feedback to that seminar was so overwhelmingly positive that I began to feel the need to start putting some of my thoughts to paper. One particular audience evaluation struck a chord with me. In it, an anonymous writer wished that she had known about ACT years ago.

That inspired me to turn the presentation into a book. Although my leadership experiences come mainly from clinical management in healthcare, the principles of leadership are universal and can be applied across a multitude of sectors. Simply put, if you are a frontline leader who needs to create positive change in a realistic and grass roots way, then this book was written with you in mind. I do not mean to deride the executives or academics that also write on this subject. In fact, chapter two details many popular and well known change theories by some very well-respected authors and speakers. My intention is not to discredit any of the other authors, but rather to present a completely different side of change management, one that actually compliments some of the other theories by going places where most have not thought to look.

From the reader's perspective, there are three types of individuals who will read this book:

1) <u>The Leader Who Is Thinking About Embarking On A Journey of Change</u>
   For this individual, it is my hope that this book will address the comment of the seminar attendant mentioned above, and hopefully provide a more expedited and seamless process of change.

2) <u>The Leader Who Is In The Midst Of Change and Having Difficulty</u>
   For this individual, my hope is that this book will serve as an aid in making a course correction on the journey of change. There might be strategies that could prove helpful and perhaps some ideas that might promote reflection as to what is not working and how to turn things around.

3) <u>The Leader Who Has Experienced Success In Promoting Positive Change In Their Organization</u>
   I commend this individual and hope that the concepts in this book will serve as validation for a job well done.

Simply put, my goal is to get everyone excited about change management. Some of the key themes that will be expanded upon in the chapters to come:

Visionary leadership

Dynamics of change

Character and adversity

Integrating the ACT model into you, as a leader

Assessing employee achievement and aptitude

Assessing organizational culture

Positively influencing employee behaviour change

Empowering, recognizing and performance managing your employees.

Fortunately for Nathan, the change journey ultimately took a turn for the better. Two years after his experience in the manger's meeting, he discovered that the program that he inherited had been found to have among the lowest number of grievances in the hospital, had gained recognition for having the highest operational efficiency and was developing best practices, which was making it into a centre of excellence. Employees, from achievement and ultimately service and performance, were greatly improved. How was that accomplished? By employing a very strategic and simple method of change leadership called "The ACT Model."

ACT stands for:

A—Assertive

C—Collaborative

T—Transparent

The very tone of this book is written with those three principles in mind. Assertive means we will deal with tough and controversial issues head on. Collaborative means that proven methods for assessing needs and strategizing change will be shared with the reader. Finally, transparent means that we tell it like it is. Hence the warning in the introduction: the harsh reality of change management needs to be out in the open and not camouflaged or veiled in any way.

Many who will read this book will be in positions of authority, with titles such as director, supervisor or manager. However, the term I will use to refer to you the reader will be "change leader." Change leader is more of a role than a title, and many who lead change may hold several different titles or positions. The important point is that anyone can lead change.

If you are in a position of authority in your organization, then you are a change leader. This book contains real life examples from the stories of change leaders that I have encountered over the years in my training and consulting practice. Others are examples that I have personally experienced, although these stories have been altered and de-identified. Also, real life examples from history, social science and contemporary life are interwoven into the book to illustrate certain concepts on a larger scale.

Despite the challenges involved, there are great outcomes that result from the process of change, examples of which I have weaved throughout the book as well as at the conclusion. However, before those results can be realized, the journey starts now.

Steve Mathew

CHAPTER 1

Vision & Dynamics of Change

Visionary leadership is what differentiates good leaders from great leaders. The ability to be forward thinking and see possibilities has been a hallmark trait of many well known leaders, in both the business and political realm. Visionary leaders have within them a "moral obligation" to accomplish something on behalf of others.

In regard to the warning in the introduction of this book, the question was raised: "why bother in the first place?" If we look closely at visionary leadership, we discover that what motivates a leader is a sense of duty, or a calling to serve. Much has been written on the subject of "servant leadership," which appears to be an oxymoron. However, as we will discover later, leaders who give more of themselves—in terms of time, mentoring and sacrifice—are the ones who ultimately leave the most lasting impact on the people they lead and serve.

We see examples of this in the public sector in fields such as healthcare, education and community services, fields in which the payoff may not be big in terms of salary and compensation. In such fields, however, one often has the opportunity to have a positive effect clients in need of care or services. Ultimately, any positive vision that is implemented in any organization must be intended to benefit the clients or people served by that organization. Vision is the first step on the journey of change, and it must be directed at the betterment of the client themselves.

For any change process to be successful it starts with a vision. Here are some key concepts related to vision:

- Vision must be progressive

- Visionary leaders need to have "hyper sight"

- Great visions are discovered, not created

- Vision must be shared

- Vision must upset the established order

- Vision involves taking risks

- Achieving a vision is a marathon, not a sprint

Hyper Sight

"Every block of stone has a statue inside it and it is the task of the sculptor to discover it."

Michaelangelo

Naturally, vision must be forward thinking. Related to this is the concept of hyper sight, which describes the ability to look beyond something and see possibilities that are not otherwise obvious. The Michaelangelo quote above conveys an image of the master sculptor who looks at a large boulder and sees a grand statue inside the rock. In the mind of the sculptor, the statue is already in the rock. His job is to chip away and reveal the sculpture he knows is already there.

One of my early mentors was a long-term care home administrator. She got me started in the field of geriatric healthcare, and I owe my career. Her story is nothing short of remarkable. She was brought into one particular organization to turn it around. The facility was wrought with organizational and labor management problems, as well as poor client care. Her vision was for the facility to someday be awarded "home of the year" by the parent corporation. When looking at what she inherited, one would easily draw the conclusion that her vision was unrealistic and almost unachievable. However, in a few short years she achieved it. She was able to look beyond the problems that were and see what could be.

Not only did her vision transform the entire facility, she also had hyper sight when it came to her own leadership team; she also saw what they could be. She knew their potential and developed every one of them to the point where they all became people of great influence in the industry. When she eventually retired, her retirement dinner party was a virtual who's who of people in the industry. What was even more amazing was that all of those influential people started out working under her leadership at some point in their careers.

Principles & Values

We will touch on themes such as these in chapter three, when we look at a leader's perceived genuineness and how well they bear up under pressure. Great leaders are always guided by principles. It was once said that while opinions can change with the times, principles should never change. If you look closely at leaders who have made dreadful decisions and ended up as failures, you will probably see that it began with some type of moral failure or flaw in the leader's personal character. One need only look to scandals in corporations, like Enron's in the 1990's, to see evidence of leaders caring little about the needs of stockholders and being deceitful in their dealings. It is crucial that leaders examine their core values, establishing what they believe in, and work to integrate those values into both their personal and professional life. A famous motivational speaker was quoted as saying that the most successful people he had met are those who are able to be the same person at home as they are at work.

Integrity is the ability to integrate ones values consistently throughout one's being and in all circumstances. Another speaker I recently heard made a rather profound statement, claiming that people are never in more internal conflict than when they are trying to be something they are not (paraphrased). To be perceived as authentic, one must be somewhat predictable. I can recall an experience with a former superior who claimed to have what he called "the imposter" complex. He would literally create his character based on how he wanted to be perceived. In other words, his personality drastically changed from situation to situation, as if he were assuming another persona. He believed that this contributed to his success.

Although research shows that people's personalities do change and adapt in relation to environment, his was a much more radical method than is usual. The problem it created was that the people around him never knew what to expect. He became unpredictable. The employees that worked under him never knew which personality they were going to get from day to day. One moment he was personable and the next he was hostile and manipulative. This damaged his credibility and created tremendous hostility and anxiety in the workplace.

Living The Change

A well-known rule of leadership is that people do what people see. Psychologists have described a similar concept as observational learning. When a leader develops a vision, the best way to sell that vision is to embody it every day and to "sell" that vision at every teachable moment that arises. I recall an experience with a former manager who was also a mentor for me. He was well known for his teachings on leadership and organizational dynamics. On one occasion I was in a meeting with him and another manager, debating a rather hot issue. As the discussion heated up the other manager became hostile and challenged my mentor. My mentor kept his cool, refrained from personal reaction and assertively put the other manager "in his place," effectively defusing the meeting and regaining control of the agenda. Put simply, he "walked the talk." He was very outspoken about his values, and he earned my respect by proving he could integrate them into his work and practice them in a high-pressure situation.

Thinking Big Working Small

It has been said that football is a game that is won by inches. The same can be said of leadership. We often emphasize doing big things and setting big goals, but often the smallest changes can have a big impact. Chapter 5 briefly touches on some of the writings of Malcolm Gladwell, who has been able to prove through social phenomena that large trends often start out as little changes. Leaders have to be able to do the little things well. Much of chapter 7 deals with the importance of recognition. Sometimes a little thank you note can be the difference between losing and retaining a valuable employee. The successful leader must keep the big picture in mind but always be prepared to work at the grass roots level, where change must ultimately originate. Good leaders seek teachable moments to sell their vision to their employees. Often, informal conversations or chats provide a chance to link all action back to a master plan or vision. The vision need not be articulated in grand meetings or to large audiences; sometimes a conversation with the right employee at the right time will create the necessary reaction. Kotter's 8 step change paradigm features a key step, called "creating the urgency." Sometimes, in small intimate conversations with an employee, a leader can use persuasion to help that person see why things need to change and coach that individual as to what role they can play in promoting positive change. However, in the change process everyone must be prepared to change, not just the employees. In fact it could be argued that the person who often changes the most is the change leader.

This is a radical shift in thinking. Most that embark on the change journey do so with the intent to change others with their vision. The truly effective leaders are the ones who allow their vision to change them first.

I recall the example of one health care CEO who was characterized by his employees as being very serious and unapproachable. He appeared far removed from the care of the clients in his facility and the perception among the employees was that he was concerned only with money and operational issues. During this time the organization was experiencing challenges with quality of care and poor morale. An external consultant was called in to mentor and assist the organization and to help turn it around. The CEO was expecting the consultant to tell him what he needed to do to change his employee's productivity. However, the consultant first worked on helping the CEO to change his own image. The CEO was coached by the consultant to make the following changes:

Stop wearing business suits and start dressing more casually.

Visit the front line workers more often and engage them in conversation; genuinely listen to their concerns.

Practice being more personable and less serious.

Invest in education for the employees.

Practice giving motivational pep talks to get them excited about the coming changes.

Create a forum for the front line workers to give him feedback, whether it was negative or positive.

The consultant also helped the CEO implement several new quality initiatives in the organization at the front line level by leveraging the highest functioning employees and training them as leaders. In the space of 2 years the organization underwent a remarkable improvement in employee productivity and morale. The CEO later remarked to the consultant that, at the time, he did not realize that the consultant was actually changing him too The CEO had earned credibility in the eyes of his employees. When they saw him living the change that he professed, they were more willing to buy into it and allow themselves to also be changed.

Creating The Ideal Picture

It is important for the change leader to create in his or her mind an idea of what the desired positive change will look like in the end. Studying the art of motivational speaking, I learned to begin by creating the end of a presentation and then to work backwards to create the actual content. By creating a picture of the way things ought to be, the change leader begins to gear and streamline all efforts towards achieving that picture; this occurs at an almost subconscious level.

How does one go about creating the ideal picture or vision? A good start is to begin with the stakeholders i.e. clients, consumers, and employees. What would they want in an ideal organization? Here are some points to consider:

Responsive Management

This means a leadership team that acts when issues are raised by responding as opposed to reacting. Responding implies a thoughtful approach guided by discretion whereas reacting implies more of an emotional or impulsive approach. Although leaders cannot always give answers to employees or clients on demand, they can respond. I have always been perplexed by the challenges associated with email. I have often been guilty of becoming annoyed when I took the time to craft an important email to a colleague only to have several days go by without an answer. I then begin to assume that the person is either deliberately ignoring my email or just can't be bothered. I descended further into madness by assuming that their silence is a statement that they no longer value or respect me as a colleague (in Cognitive Behavioral Therapy that type of cognitive distortion is often referred to as mind reading or making assumptions). I then run into my colleague in the workplace and finally ask why they did not get back to my email. They then answer that they have been busy and have not found the time to read it.

That entire situation could have been avoided if my colleague had done one simple thing, respond. They did not have to write a detailed dissertation of a response but simply needed to send a quick reply saying "got your email, I am bogged down right now but will get back to you by_____." This is a good example of responding. By doing so we validate the person, which is almost as important, if not more important, than answering the actual message. In writing this, I declare myself a complete hypocrite, as I know that I have missed responding to some of my colleague's emails and I probably frustrated them just as much. However, it is still important to validate even if we slip up.

Employees and clients want change leaders who will take the time to validate them and their concerns. I recall several times coming into work and finding my employees upset and in crisis due to being short staffed or some other concern. Even though I might have an important meeting to get to, I would often stop and take three-to-five minutes to let them vent, acknowledge the concern and help them channel complaining into problem solving. I saw this as a proactive investment. If I had done the opposite, if I had reacted emotionally or dismissed their concerns outright and then headed off to my meeting, I would have paid the price later on. The complaint would have festered and boiled into a bigger problem and probably would have created a lot of resentment later on.

Much has been written about applying this approach when dealing with clients from a customer service perspective. If a client or stakeholder brings a concern to a change leader and expects an answer, then the change leader should definitely acknowledge the concern, explore the issue, and at the very least promise to investigate and set a follow up meeting or phone call.

A High Morale Workplace

What exactly is morale? It can be thought of as the "emotional climate" of an organization. It is completely subjective and cannot be quantified or measured in objective terms. Morale can be measured by assessing both the physical environment of an organization, the interactions between employees and clients, as well as employees' oral behaviors. To illustrate, let's go back to a customer service example. Imagine how you would feel if you walked into a place of business and observed the following:

- A sloppy and disorganized environment.
- A phone ringing and no one answering it.
- The person at the reception desk rolling their eyes and being discourteous to customers.
- Every time you go to speak to someone they either ignore you or walk away.
- The employees have miserable looks on their faces and defensive body language.

How would you rate the morale in that organization? Just by scanning the environment you can gather significant information that can help you determine whether or not you want to do business there.

On the other hand, what if you walked into another organization and saw evidence of the following:

- A welcoming and secure feeling.
- Happy and well-cared for clients.
- Trained and caring employees who appear to go above and beyond the call of duty.
- Respectful and courteous behavior towards everyone.
- Plaques, awards and photos indicating that organization's good reputation in the community.

How would you rate the morale in that organization compared to the first? Every change leader wants to reap the benefits of a high-morale workplace. A high morale workplace means productivity, happy employees, a client-centered focus and efficiency. It also means greater recruitment and higher retention. Morale is often measured by employee satisfaction surveys. The change leader can rely on this information to track progress as the change process unfolds, and then celebrate successes with employees, clients and other stakeholders.

Where To Focus Change

Although the terms leadership and management are used interchangeably, the following Venn diagram illustrates the similarities and differences between the terms.

Management refers to processes and operational duties such as:

    Recruitment

    Budget

    Equipment and supplies

- Physical plant and environment

- Employee scheduling

- Payroll

Leadership refers to people and includes duties like:

- Team meetings

- Individual performance appraisals

- Goal setting

- Performance management

- Empowerment

- Education

At leadership management seminars, I sometimes ask the audience to indicate which of the two roles outline above presents the most challenges and struggles. Unanimously, the audience always responds with the people side of the equation. Most leaders/managers can learn how to manage a budget, order supplies etc. The bigger problems include efforts to motivate employees and dealing with resistance or conduct issues. In one management seminar on dealing with employee performance, I was in a room with managers from a variety of sectors, including business, retail, and social services, to name a few. When it came to discussing problem employee behavior, it was amazing how similar the stories were. The behaviors described, and their impact on the managers and organizations, were identical, despite the wide array of work environments represented at the seminar.

Pareto says that 80% of a problem can be solved by identifying and concentrating efforts on the key 20% of issues. Demings furthered Pareto when he stated that 80% of problems in an organization are caused by systems and process whereas 20% care caused by people.

Change must happen by getting results through the employee. Thus, the concept of "buy in" and motivation becomes important, and will be addressed later. Japanese Kaizen leadership strongly advocates for involving and engaging the frontline employee in the process of quality improvement. Engaging the front line employee is critical to helping to identify wastage, excessive handoffs of tasks between employees and poor productivity.

Why Change At All?

The process of change may be initiated by 3 conditions or circumstances:

- Crisis

- New governmental demands

- Innovation

For example, the tragic events of September 11, 2001 forever changed airport security and international travel. Or, the Sudden Acute Respiratory Syndrome (SARS) outbreak in 2003 heightened the awareness of infection control in public places, beyond just hospitals and clinics.

Change creates uncertainty, confusion, searching, and, often, conflict. People will inevitably feel:

- Uncomfortable and self-conscious.

- A sense of loss or grief.

- Isolated, even if everyone else is going through the change.

Often, new demands such as government policy changes or legislations can be the impetus for change. The recent explosion of technology and information has also driven change to the point that virtually every workplace is now somehow connected or reliant on computers. One health care organization that transitioned to a computerized documentation system serves as a good illustration of this point. Prior to the new system going live, there were several retirement notices from senior employees. These workers admitted to not having the technological forte of the younger workers, who email and text as easily as they walk. Change can be dramatic and can radically change the workplace, as well as its traditions and culture.

The Change Leader Role

Leading change in the face of such circumstances is no easy task. The change leader is tasked with building a new vision of how things can be done better. This also involves translating the vision into an agenda, and communicating that agenda. The change leader must also create an environment of collaboration, giving the employees as much power and control as possible to implement small changes in their own individual areas. The more control employees have over their environment, the higher their level of job satisfaction. Creating an environment of ongoing problem solving is fundamental to successfully implementing change. Suggestion boxes, surveys and informal focus groups are all ways of getting employees to "buy in" to new ideas. The change leader must also be persistent. If procrastination thrives or if no visible progress is made, then employees will often return to the status quo, because it is familiar and safe.

Change leaders must also be honest enough to inform their teams that every process of change involves "bugs" in the system and will therefore require adjustments and corrections to be made, until the process flows smoothly. Acknowledging and communicating problems before they happen helps to alleviate the anxiety associated with change and to put employees more at ease. As the process of change moves ahead, the change leader must be prepared to coach and mentor those who demonstrate leadership abilities, and must be prepared to delegate responsibilities as much as possible.

Change Is An Unpopular Concept

It is a given that people can only handle so much change. Too much change, too soon, inevitably causes change fatigue. Therefore, change leaders must know how to pace change. Often, change leaders themselves are at the mercy of corporate timelines and limited funding. This creates tremendous pressure to implement a lot of change in a small amount of time. If this is the case, then the change leader must be prepared to advocate for employees and communicate issues like employee burnout to senior leadership. At times, the change leader must be ready to negotiate deadlines on behalf of the employees. If this is successful, it helps to build the change leader's credibility and demonstrate sensitivity and empathy to the employees.

Different people will always display a range of readiness for change. In preparing for a team-building session, I came across an interesting six sigma exercise that involves people pairing up and then turning away to change their appearance in subtle ways. When the partners turn around again they each must then guess what the other changed about their appearance. I once used this exercise in a presentation. The main point was not the accuracy with which people noticed their partner's change but how they responded to the exercise itself. For example, some of those who did the exercise were very excited and enthusiastic. Those individuals jumped right into the exercise and typically laughed and had fun changing their appearance with their partners. Some individuals were noticeably uncomfortable with the exercise. Their body language clearly communicated that they were uncomfortable or embarrassed at having to change their appearance. These individuals were noticeably hesitant and tended to look around the room looking very unsure, but they eventually did it and many ended up actually enjoying the exercise. Another small group of individuals outright refused to participate. They remained in their seats and typically crossed their arms to clearly convey by their body language that they were clearly not interested.

These reactions demonstrate what I call the "Change Continuum," illustrated below:

Enthusiast   Skeptic   Overt Resister   Covert Saboteur

The Covert Saboteur is added to the continuum as a toxic resister. This individual is not easily detected and is usually revealed as change progresses. This individual is typically passive aggressive and may initially look as though they are agreeing with the need for change. However, behind the scenes they are actively engaged in sabotaging the change leader. Regardless, change leaders need to be prepared for the fact that employees can fall anywhere on the change continuum, and so must plan accordingly. The enthusiast needs to be tapped for their energy, the skeptic needs evidence and time to be convinced, the overt resister needs to be confronted tactfully and disarmed by channeling their negative energy from complaining to problem solving, and the covert saboteur needs to be exposed. We will discuss more about this concept in upcoming chapters.

Lack Of Resources

A typical response from many employees is that they lack the resources to successfully implement change. Although that may be true at times, if one waited until all the resources were in place, change would never occur. In fact sometimes the most profound change happens when there is scarcity or lack of resources.

What do the following items have in common?

>Scotch tape

>Analog computer

>FM radio

>Drive-in movies

>Jet engine

The answer is that they were all invented in the 1930's, during the Great Depression. Just because things were scarce, that did not stop individuals with ingenuity and vision to accomplish great things. I once heard a very popular speaker make a comment that sometimes having all the resources we need creates mediocrity. Excellence often comes during times of being under resourced, because it forces the change leader to find creative solutions and to find resources in places they would not normally seek them. IBM was launched into greatness during the Great Depression of the 1930's because there was a need for data machines. The result was their domination of the IT market for 50 years, and it all started at a time when most corporations were going out of business.

Building Momentum

Momentum is critical to sustaining change. Change must be implemented at "pedal to the metal" pace, and it must be continuous. The moment change leaders take their foot off the gas, employees will return to the familiar and the status quo, because it is safe, predictable and easier, at least in their perception. Many employees reject change because what is proposed is seen to violate their expected traditions, norms and values.

In the field of psychiatry and mental health, a common practice decades ago was the practice of performing a psychosurgery, known as lobotomy, on patients with various forms of schizophrenia. By severing connections in the frontal lobe of the brain, it was believed that these individuals would become less dangerous and more placid. What it actually did was make many of these people vegetative, while leaving others with permanent features like flattened affect, apathy and lack of motivation. Others showed signs of dis-inhibited behaviors (which are socially unacceptable) and euphoria. The number of lobotomies began to decrease rapidly in the 1970's, as the practice was found to be inhumane and to lack the empirical evidence needed to prove any significant improvement the procedure induced in patients.

Today in mental health, there are far better treatments involving psychopharmacology and psychotherapies that are evidence based and have been proven to increase the quality of life for individuals with severe psychiatric disorders.

Perception Of Loss & Discomfort

However, whenever there is change, there is also a fear of loss and the accompanying grief. You might wonder what grief has to do with this discussion. Grief occurs whenever there is a perceived loss. If the individual believes that they are losing something, then they often go through some or all of Kubler-Ross's stages of grief, which include denial, blame, bargaining, anger, depression and acceptance.

Reference: Kübler-Ross, E. (1969) *On Death and Dying*, Routledge

Case Example

Linda held a position as an activity aide helping clients learn life skills. The organization decided that best practices involved all employees engaging in life skills training for clients, which made Linda's job redundant. She was then informed that she would be expected to perform other duties as well. Linda responded initially by telling colleagues that the organization would never change her role, as she was far too valuable. However, the organization eventually met with her to officially tell her that the role was being eliminated. She tried to bargain in an attempt to keep her job, but she was unsuccessful.

Her demeanor then changed as she began to blame the change leader. She outwardly expressed her anger about the decision to her colleagues, insinuating that she was entitled to the role, given her many years of service. She eventually took a sick leave for 3 months due to depression and stress. She never actually moved to the acceptance stage of grieving and eventually became a bitter employee.

Try this:

Cross your arms.

Now cross your arms again, this time changing your arms in the opposite position.

How does that feel?

This illustrates the point that changes in uncomfortable. However, if you really put your mind to it and trained yourself to cross your arms the opposite way, you could probably condition yourself to permanently change the way you cross your arms. People do have the capacity to work through changes, learn and adapt. In fact, people never change for the better when they are comfortable.

Chances are that if you look at some of the most successful individuals in the world, they probably got that way by taking risks and pushing themselves out of their comfort zones. On a personal note, my natural personality style is introverted and task-focused. I once took a personality seminar where I had to identify my opposite type (i.e. the one that is least like me), and that turned out to be outgoing and people-oriented. I learned later that the trait that was the least associated with me was actually my hidden key to success. When I began to take speaking engagements, my natural inclination was to lecture and present the content in a very linear and fact-based way. However, one of my mentors taught me about the importance of being dynamic and engaging with an audience. I then began to adapt my speaking style to be more outgoing and captivating. To this day, this change in strategy has brought me most of my success and professional fulfillment.

The irony is that my wife, Denise, actually possesses my opposite personality style (extroverted and people oriented), which explains why opposites attract in a marriage. One time Denise attended one of my workshops and when the people at the table found out she was my wife they naturally asked: "Is he this dynamic and outgoing at home?" Denise almost fell off her chair laughing. Her response was that her husband was the exact opposite at home. Similarly, any change leader must be prepared to go where they would rather not go and to push themselves in ways they never thought imaginable. Only then can they realize their true potential; many often surprise themselves as they discover talents and abilities they never knew they had.

Finally, another main cause of resistance to change is the belief that change is a form of criticism of the way things have always been done. This is a difficult obstacle to overcome. As we have seen, change touches people at a very personal level and can create any number of emotional responses. The change leader must be sensitive to—and acknowledge and validate—the good practices and traditions that have occurred in a given organization, and leaders must make it known that their vision is to build the next layer on top of the good foundations that already exist. This also underscores the point that the change leader must not only validate traditions and processes, he or she must also validate people. As we will see in later chapters, recognition of value are arguably the highest needs of any employee. Change leader must find ways to engage people and value them if they wish to motivate and empower employees to embrace positive change.

Review Of Key Principles

Vision is what distinguishes great leaders.

During the change process, the person who changes most is the change leader.

Deming's Law states 80% of problems in an organization are caused by systems and process and 20% by people.

The more control employees have over their environment, the higher their level of job satisfaction.

Sometimes the most profound change happens when there is scarcity or a lack of resources.

Change leaders need to be prepared for the fact that employees can fall anywhere on the continuum of change, and must plan accordingly.

People have to allow themselves to be made uncomfortable in order to be challenged and to grow.

The ACT of Change Management

MDM: ACT MODEL OF CHANGE MANAGEMENT

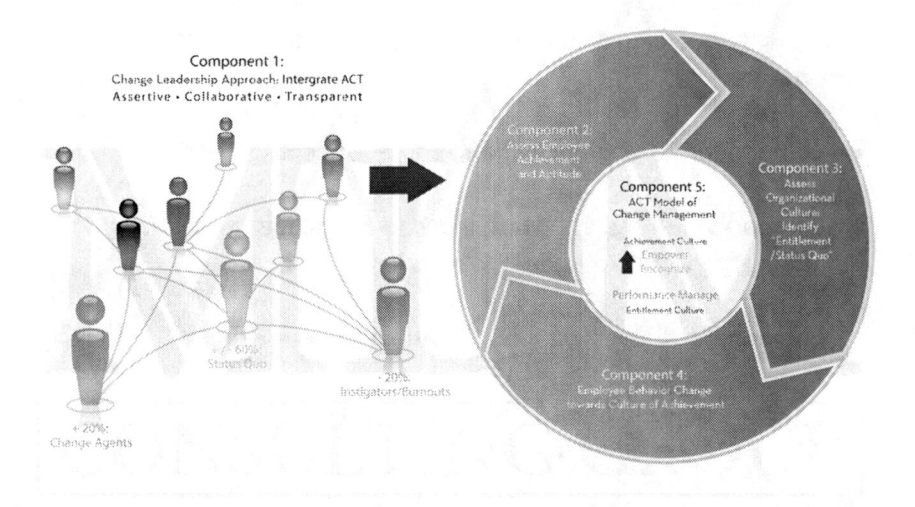

Component 1:
Change Leadership Approach: Intergrate ACT
Assertive • Collaborative • Transparent

+ 20%:
Change Agents

60%
Status Quo

20%
Instigators/Burnouts

Component 2:
Assess Employee
Achievement
and Aptitude

Component 3:
Assess
Organizational
Culture:
Identify
"Entitlement
/Status Quo"

Component 5:
ACT Model of
Change Management

Achievement Culture
Empower
Recognize

Performance Manage:
Entitlement Culture

Component 4:
Employee Behavior Change
towards Culture of Achievement

Assertive • Collaborative • Transparent

© MDM Consulting Group not to be reproduced without permission

CHAPTER 2

CHANGE MODELS & ACT

The ACT Model Of Change Management: Being The Change

The ACT Model involves 5 components, which will be expanded upon throughout upcoming chapters. The components the change leader must carry out are:

Component 1) Integrate ACT into you, as the change leader.

Component 2) Assess your individual employee's by looking at achievement and aptitude.

Component 3) Assess your organization's culture.

Component 4) Influence employee behavior change to become a culture of achievement.

Component 5) Empower, recognize and performance manage.

Up to this point we have set the foundation of the ACT model by discussing the importance of vision and understanding the dynamics associated with change. In the introduction of this book, reference was made to the numerous change models around today. Many of those models possess great credibility and proven strategies that help in promoting organizational change. It is important to review these models in order to understand the way in which the ACT model both contrasts and complements many of these models, which include:

Pareto: 80/20 Principle

Kotter: 8 Step Change Model

Kouzes & Posner: 5 Practices of Exemplary Leaders

Gladwell: The Tipping Point

Positive Psychology: Focusing on Strengths

Appreciative Inquiry: Environment of Collaborative Problem Solving

Pareto & People Investment

Perhaps the greatest and most proven model for understanding change comes from Vilfredo Pareto. The Pareto Principle, or 80/20 rule, was first developed by Pareto, an Italian Economist, in late 1800's and early 1900's. Pareto discovered that 80% of the wealth in Italy was attributed to only 20% of the population, who were primarily rich landowners. Pareto also found similar patterns in other European countries, which revealed the concept of unequal distribution. This same pattern was expanded on in the field of sociology, and similar trends of unequal distribution were found to be woven throughout the fabric of society, often in areas not necessarily related to economics. For example:

> 80% of the traffic in most cities drives on 20% of the roadways.
>
> 80% of our clothes come from only 20% of the clothes we wear in our closets (the same is probably true of shoes).
>
> 80% of daily productivity comes from only 20% of your day (this applies to time management).
>
> 80% of team productivity comes from 20% of meeting time.
>
> 80% of the phone calls we make are to only 20% of the people in our personal phone directory.
>
> 80% of management headaches come from the same 20% of people.

Simply put, the Pareto principle states that there is an imbalance between inputs and outputs. We often think that input equals output, but that is not necessarily true. How often do we put 100% effort into something that ends up yielding a disappointing result? So for the purposes of change management, 80% of productivity results from 20% of effort.

<u>Change Management Application</u>

We also know that the change leader must know how to invest in people to produce that positive change. A typical trap that most of us fall into is the belief that we need to change everybody, or the majority, in order to produce positive change. That is not true. A change agent who understands Pareto will also know that investing in the correct 20% of people will yield an 80% change. In chapter four we will look more closely into this issue.

Kotter & "Operationalizing Change"

Dr. John Kotter (Kotter and Cohen, 2002) surveyed numerous organizations and companies and found that 70% of all change efforts in organizations ultimately fail. Kotter also found that the organizations that were able to achieve and sustain positive change all had several things in common, which he developed into an 8 step model:

1. Create the urgency
2. Build the guiding team
3. Develop the vision
4. Communicate to get buy-in
5. Remove obstacles
6. Create short term wins
7. Persist and don't give up
8. Make the change sustainable.

<u>Change Management Application</u>

The strength of Kotter's model is that it breaks the process of change down into 8 simplified steps. This is ideal for the development of committees and teams meant to steer positive change in most organizations.

Leadership Credibility: Kouzes & Posner

In their book *The Leadership Challenge*, James Kouzes and Barry Posner (2007) developed the "Five Practices of Exemplary Leaders." Their hypothesis challenges the belief that leadership is based on personality. Instead, they posit that exemplary leadership is based on five effective leadership practices, such as:

1. Model the Way
2. Inspire a Shared Vision
3. Challenge the Process
4. Enable Others to Act
5. Encourage the Heart.

Change Management Application

The strength of Kouzes and Posner's work is that it puts the onus of personal responsibility and self-reflection on the change leader. The change leader models the change that is needed and also develops positive change in other leaders. This model also challenges the change leader to develop credibility first, before considering how they can positively impact others.

Gladwell & 20% Critical Mass

The Tipping Point is a captivating book written by reporter Malcolm Gladwell (2002). He deals with social change and how certain trends can spread quickly, like epidemics. The "Tipping Point" occurs when a given variable reaches 20% critical mass; it is then that change may happen suddenly. This debunks the notion that change takes a long time. Although some processes of change may take years, small changes that happen spontaneously can result in big changes in the long run. Gladwell uses examples like the resurgence of Hush Puppy shoes, which became popular again when people in Manhattan started wearing them, spurring a trend that spread rapidly throughout the rest of the US. He also talks about television programs like Sesame Street; he focuses on how that show challenged traditional beliefs about children and educational media and created an entirely new way of educating children, which is still used today.

In fact, as I write this, my children have been raving about these trendy elastic bands which are shaped like famous people and interesting objects. The new trend is that kids in the neighborhood collect them and trade them in the schoolyards. The other day my eight and eleven-year-old came home insisting that my wife go out and purchase these bands because "everybody" was wearing them at school. My wife then spent the better part of an afternoon searching every store in the area, only to find they were almost sold out. What was interesting was that I never once saw a television advertisement for these things, which one could purchase at a 99 cent store. This example proves that many social changes start with word of mouth and can spread like an epidemic.

Change Management Application

It is critically important for any change leader to be aware that small changes often make a big difference in the long run. The change leader needs to know how to build that 20% critical mass if the organization is going to tip towards positive change.

Tuckman & Team Development Bruce Tuckman's stages of team development have long been considered the gold standard for measuring growth in an organization (Tuckman & Jensen, 1977). Tuckman's model of team development includes four main stages, with an additional fifth stage:

1. Forming
2. Norming
3. Storming
4. Performing
5. (Adjourning)

As the team moves from stage one to stage four, it moves from being disorganized, with members challenging each other for power, to being autonomous, achievement-oriented and highly productive. At the same time, the leader's role moves from directing to delegating. In other words, as the team starts to step up, the leader starts to step back and the team develops self-governance. During the fifth stage, adjourning, the team begins to dissolve and people part ways for positive reasons, i.e. professional growth and/or project completion.

Change Management Application

Change leaders can use Tuckman's stages to help anticipate obstacles and negative group behaviors as they implement their change plan. Change leaders can also use the Tuckman criteria to evaluate their team's progress, according to the stage they are on.

Positive Psychology: Strength-Based Approach

Martin Seligman is one of the main proponents of this recent psychology paradigm that challenges the traditional problem-based approach to understanding and shaping human behavior. Positive psychology attempts to build on a person's strengths and virtues, instead of on their limitations. Themes like flow, mindfulness, positive self-talk, as well as an environment of praise and positive reinforcement, are emphasized.

Change Management Application

The change leader must be able to see strengths in even the most toxic resistors and work towards giving those people opportunities to improve.

Appreciative Inquiry: Focusing On What Works

Engagement with employees moves change forward. Appreciative inquiry seeks to create a collaborative learning environment that focuses on what works, instead of focusing solely on solving problems. Like positive psychology, this method focuses on strengths. Questions are asked to help the group envision the future while valuing individual contributions to change. Exercises such as brainstorming draw people in to generate ideas and foster positive relationships.

Change Management Application

The change leader must be able to create a learning environment that engages employees and constantly reinforces education, skill building and design improvement.

The ACT Model Of Change Management

After reviewing all the previous models, it is clear that many of them have strong credibility and have proven to be quite effective in either contributing to or actively promoting positive change. However, when one looks deeper, the majority of these models share one thing in common: they are almost always focused on the leader "doing" something. For example, Kotter's model is an excellent step by step process to steer change. However, if the change leader has serious character flaws and is not trustworthy, it is not guaranteed that he or she will get past step 4. Similarly, Kouzes and Posner's 5 Practices model emphasizes the leader's modeling, inspiring, challenging, enabling and encouraging. These are all noble pursuits; however, again, they focus on the change leader "doing." Modeling, inspiring, challenging, enabling and encouraging must originate somewhere; they do not develop in a vacuum. If the change leader is someone who traditionally does the opposite of the 5 exemplary practices, and then suddenly started employing them, it would likely raise a few eyebrows.

So the question no one seems to be asking concerns where these practices come from and how a change leader acquires them. The answer is that the above mentioned models posit a moral framework that originates from within an individual's character. These are not just external practices or traits.

What a person does stems from who that person is. When considering famous leaders who have "fallen from grace" in the public eye, their fall can almost always be traced back to a moral failure that started with that person's character. Conversely, the most successful leaders of change were not perfect people but people who had great strength of character and principles that were never compromised. This is not intended to sound overly moralistic, implying that a change leader must be perfect in every way. However, character counts. As much as we need to build new skills and employ different methods to achieve positive change, it is equally important to ensure that we explore and develop our own character first. Before people accept the change process, they must first accept the change leader.

Notice that one does not *do* assertiveness, nor can they *do* collaboration or transparency. Rather, they must *be* assertive, *be* collaborative and *be* transparent with all their employees in order to model positive change.

Once a change leader focuses on being, then doing things like creating a vision, acquiring short terms wins, modeling the way forward, overcoming obstacles and enabling others will flow more naturally. Thus, the ACT model of change management compliments many of the other change models by presenting a balanced view of change management that focuses on the developing internal character of the leader and the leaders around them before implementing external changes. The credibility and character of the change leader is a higher predictor of success than is the change model that is used.

The Introspective Leader

ACT requires the change leader to be able to look within, challenging one to carefully examine one's own character and principles. The ACT Model of Change Management is about what the leader brings to the table, not just about what process the leader uses, as laid out in the leadership Venn diagram "inspiring people to follow you," above. Ultimately, people follow the change leader, not just the change process.

Writing about Sir Winston Churchill, former US Secretary of State Henry Kissinger commented on the difference between a hero and a superstar. To paraphrase, he stated that superstars strive for public approval and applause, while heroes walk alone. Superstars see success as a means to gain support, while heroes strive for success as an outgrowth of their inner values.

The Authentic Leader

In "Discovering your Authentic Leadership" (George, et al., 2007), the authors claim that leaders are considered trustworthy when they are authentic and do not try to be someone else. In a recent workshop, I asked the audience to think about a manager or supervisor who they enjoyed working with in the past and to think about why they felt that way about the person. Almost unanimously the audience agreed that the biggest reason that they liked that person was because they saw them as authentic. I also recall seeing the results of an employee satisfaction survey in one organization, in which the employees were asked about the quality most important to them in their managers. That quality was trust, and in order to be trusted one must first be perceived as authentic.

Leaders must be passionate. If the change leader is not passionate about change, then their employees will not be either. Change leaders must be able to "sell the vision" constantly and wear their passion on their sleeve. Passion is both contagious and inspiring. Change leaders are continually told to "not take things personally" when they encounter push back from their employees. This is easier said than done, because I believe this is directly related to passion. Passion is a double-edged sword. On one hand, the high energy and emotion generated by passion motivates change leaders to overcome obstacles and to achieve great things. The downside is that when things do not turn out the way the change leader wants, it is equally crushing and disappointing. To ask the change leader to not take things personally, then, is to literally ask them to quench their own passion. This is a common trait among high performance athletes. Their passion enables them to perform at a level that few can reach. However, these same individuals take losing very hard and can never be comfortable with mediocrity. Instead of telling a change leader not to take failure personally, a more realistic perspective is to help them accept the fact that the higher the achievement aimed at, the higher the potential fall, because there is always the potential for failure. The change leader should anticipate pitfalls and develop a strong social network; the change leader should also learn from failure and develop coping skills to be deployed during difficult periods in order to rebound with strength and energy.

Teachable Moments

Authentic leaders are able to lead with their heads and their hearts, which means they must be able to invest in their employees. In order to do so, they must focus on building relationships. These investments often occur in everyday interactions. Every conversation, whether it is formal or informal, can become an opportunity for a teachable moment in which the change leader can "sell" the vision. Often, the most profound changes come from spontaneous conversations between change leaders and their employees.

For example, if an organization is moving toward excellence in service delivery or operational efficiency, a skilled change leader can find ways to weave those themes into regular conversations with employees, as illustrated below.

Issue To Discuss With Employee	Change Leader Opportunity To Coach, Engage And Link Lesson To The Vision
Employee: Julie Issue: Chronic lateness	"Julie, I have noticed that you have been demonstrating a pattern of arriving late to work. I want you to know that **as part of our new operational vision we are striving to ensure punctuality for all our employees.** Maybe you could help us with some suggestions towards supporting employees who are having difficulty making it to work on time?"
Employee: Ronald Issue: Communication	"Ronald, I see that you requested a shift exchange with your colleague at the last minute. I want to remind you that these need to be approved by me first. As part of our new vision we are considering **implementing a computerized scheduling system.** This will allow employees to input shift exchange requests that I can check and track to avoid any miscommunications."
Employee: Brenda Issue: Problem solving	"Brenda, I have noticed that you seem to get frustrated when you feel there is no solution to a problem you are struggling with. **One of my goals is to help my leaders develop creative problem solving skills.** I would like us both to think about the problem and each come up with 3 potential solutions and then meet again to review them together."

The workplace is about relationships. It is arguable that every change leader strives to establish a relationship with each employee on an everyday basis. A colleague once asked me about a former colleague of mine, who had since been promoted. The colleague asked me if my former colleague ever asked me about what was going on in my personal life. She then went on to say that my former colleague never appeared concerned about her on a personal level, and that that bothered her. It made me think that every change leader must get to know their people on a personal level. This enables the change leader to connect with each employee, thus valuing them. The bottom line is that your employees need to know that you genuinely care about them personally, not just professionally.

I recall reading a well known book on public speaking and the author made this point (paraphrased): The speaker must make an effort to build a relationship with every member of that audience during that presentation. I would propose to apply that same principle to change management and state that every change leader's daily responsibility is to connect and establish relationships with their employees.

Check-Ins

Many are familiar with the following acronym "MBWA," which stands for management by walking around. There is much credibility to this concept. I have heard many employees in organizations complain that their managers mostly sits behind their desk and do not bother to interact with the employees. Most managers would respond by saying that they would like to engage more with employees, but seldom get the opportunity to because they have so much paperwork and deadlines to meet. However, the onus is on the manager to change the employee's perception. If the employees already have a "management vs. us" mentality, then it is up to the manager to change that perception.

One of the ways the change leader can do this is by actually scheduling regular check-ins throughout the day. In my practice as a manager, I always attempted to walk through the employees work area at least three times a day: in the morning, at midday and at the end of the day. At times I really had no reason to do this and sometimes I did not make it obvious that I was observing the employees; sometimes I went to an empty desk and made a phone call to check my voicemail or made up an excuse like needing to shred a document. I noticed that being visible created opportunities for me to deal with problems on the spot as they occurred. In fact, the more available I was, the more often I was present when problems surfaced, and this created an opportunity to collaborate with my employees and problem solve as a team. Being visible and available also gave employees the opportunity to grab me and ask me questions. Often, employees were too shy and would hesitate to initiate a conversation, but seeing me often gave them the chance to pull me aside and share their thoughts or feelings. I also noticed that it gave me the opportunity to engage in small talk and ask the employees how they were doing. As change leader, you should make it a point to know at least 2-3 things about each of your employees, in terms of family life, interests, as well as things like hobbies and places they liked to vacation.

<u>Exercise</u>

In the spaces below, write down the names of 10 of your employees. Then write 2-3 facts about that person that would help you start a conversation the next time you see them. Make sure that you don't only write the names of positive employees; also include some of your most negative employees.

1.

2.

3.

4.

5.

6.

7.

8.

9.

10.

Now the challenge is to use that information the next time you encounter these employees. Also, don't be afraid to engage those negative employees. They may question your motives but you will find that building a relationship actually disarms them. Showing genuine kindness and compassion towards them often creates conflicting emotions, i.e. it goes against the perception they have of you. A rule of thumb here is that in order for employees to create animosity between themselves and their leader, they must first create a perception of distance from that leader allowing them to alienate the leader. Most managers unknowingly reinforce this pattern by avoiding conflict and remaining aloof from negative employees, when in actuality, the effective change leader is the one who boldly walks right into the lion's den and dares to invade the territory of the negative employees.

I found it very amusing whenever I would walk into the employee's lunchroom. The conversations would suddenly cease and heads would automatically go down. At first it felt awkward as I would take out my lunch container and place it in the microwave. I would then leave, feeling as if I was invading the "employee's turf." After a while I decided to change my strategy. One time, I walked into the employees lounge and the conversations died down, but I decided to draw attention to it. As I was getting ready to warm up my lunch, I jokingly stated to the employees: "I notice you guys stop talking when I enter the lunchroom. It's okay, you can finish calling me an SOB after I leave." At first there was dead silence, then one by one they started to crack up laughing. The ice was broken and before too long they were inviting me to sit down and have lunch with them.

The Power Of Proximity

Continuing with the theme of distance and the space between individuals, I remember a former colleague who was an experienced consultant. Often he had to provide reports to powerful and influential people in senior management positions. He gave me a great piece of advice concerning such meetings: never allow them to sit behind their desk when you give your report. I asked why and he said it was because the desk symbolizes power and acts as a barrier between you and them. If you sit across from them and they are behind their desk, you are essentially sitting in the role of an employee, and before you know it you will end up feeling like a subordinate, because they will subconsciously treat you as one.

I took this a step further when dealing with another issue in an organization in which I worked. The controller for this organization was a well known and notorious micro-manager. His office was actually beside the employee's washroom. Believe it or not, the controller was keeping track of how often each employee used the washroom, because it was not productive time This same individual was even meticulous about how the date was written on proposals and reports, as well as what font had to be used. I remember sitting in his office reviewing a proposal I had written and, sure enough, I noticed that he was behind his desk.

I remember walking out of that meeting feeling very angry, resentful and insulted at the way he treated me. So, the next time I tried something different. While we were in his office for the next meeting, I pulled my chair from around the desk and parked it right beside him on his side of the desk. He froze in place, save for his eyes darting around the room. By the end of the meeting he was much more polite.

I do not recommend this strategy to those reading this book. It was clearly a risky thing to do, but the experiment did prove a point about the power of proximity, distance and body language. For a negative person to intimidate others, they must create distance and put up barriers. A positive change leader who seeks to break down barriers can sometimes do so by literally moving closer to that person and forcing them to interact with you. The meta message you give them is that you are not afraid to engage them up close. If you can combine this with some social conversation with them, it might also serve to disarm them and give you the opportunity to demonstrate that you are genuine and authentic, which would help to change their perception of you.

ACT In Contrast To Other Change Models

Earlier in the chapter we examined many other change models. The ACT Model of Change Management compliments these models as illustrated in the chart below:

Other Change Model "DOING"	ACT Model Of Change Management "BEING"
Pareto	Empower the 20% of high achievement and aptitude employees to be change agents.
Kotter	Employ ACT Model as the overarching strategy and then operationalize it using the 8 steps with the 20% who become the guiding team.
Kouzes & Posner	Provide balance by adding the importance of the inner character of the change leader, which brings even more credibility to the 5 exemplary practices.
Gladwell	ACT focuses change by empowering the positive 20% of employees in an organization. Those 20% of positive employees constitute the 20% critical mass necessary for circumstances to tip towards positive change.
Tuckman	The 5 stages can be used as a gauge to measure whether ACT is making an impact on team functioning.
Positive Psychology	ACT builds on each employee's strengths and raises the bar on their limitations through a collaborative process.
Appreciative Inquiry	ACT promotes knowledge to practice by investing in the intellectual capital of the 20% of positive employees who become change agents. They generate the ideas that drive change.

Review Of Key Principles

Other change models are based on the change leader doing things differently. The ACT model of change management presents another view of change management, which entails the change leader being the change and not just doing change.

In order to be successful as a change leader, he or she must be introspective and able to look within in order to examine their own character. They must also be authentic.

Before people will accept a change process, they must first accept the change leader.

The change leader must also be very relationship focused and make attempts to connect with their employees on an everyday basis. They must also actively sell their vision through everyday opportunities and interactions. This also applies to the most negative resistors.

The temptation of the change leader is to avoid the negative resistor, but an effective change leader is aware that engagement at close proximity can be used to disarm even the most toxic of employees.

The goal is not to be a perfect leader but to be a balanced leader.

CHAPTER 3

INTEGRATE ACT INTO YOU, AS THE CHANGE LEADER

The first component of the ACT Model begins with the change leader being assertive, collaborative and transparent in every situation. In this chapter we will delve deeper in those three qualities, in addition to exploring the importance of the change leader's ability to persevere through adversity. We will also gain a better understanding of where each person in your organization falls on the change continuum.

Integrity

Recall that integrity can be thought of a person's ability to integrate their values into their entire being. One of the biggest pitfalls a leader can fall prey to is being perceived as a hypocrite. I recall the story of one well known company president who was famous for preaching empowerment and positive organizational dynamics. The problem was that the employees in his own organization described him as a dictator who was ruthless, cruel and manipulative. He ended up leaving a trail of broken and wounded people behind him, many of whom ended up quitting. He was a prime example of "do as I say, not as I do." This leader was overly concerned with making sure that he was perceived as powerful and always in control, at all times and in all situations.

Although it is always important for a leader to remain in control, especially during a crisis, that does not mean that he or she should be afraid of being vulnerable around their employees. In fact, the opposite is true. It is more important that a change leader be perceived as "real," as opposed to powerful.

Being real means that the change leader is not afraid to show their humanity or express their emotions to their employees. In fact, polls have been taken on political elections and, in many cases, it has been proven that the more the public can relate to a candidate on a personal level, the more likely it is that that candidate will have success in an election.

In fact, in the town hall meetings held during recent presidential campaigns, the candidates usually did not wear a suit jacket. They usually wore a dress shirt and tie with the sleeves rolled up. The suit jacket is considered formal attire, while the more casual look, with the sleeves rolled up, gives the public the impression that they are ready to work and to get their hands dirty, so to speak. Again, this is based on creating an image and a public perception. As we saw in the previous chapter, the workplace is all about relationships. It is important that the change leader be perceived as personable and relatable to their employees, in addition to being grounded in reality.

Assertiveness

Take a look at the following scenarios and indicate how you would most likely respond:

1. Your neighbor has more garbage bags than he is allowed on pickup day. To avoid being charged more for the extra bags, he has started leaving some of his garbage bags on your curb since the number of your bags is typically less than his. However, he does not ask your permission to do this. How would you respond?

    a) Remove the bag and put it back on your neighbor's lawn along with a nasty note.
    b) Go over to your neighbor's house and politely ask to speak to him and clarify that you don't mind helping him out, but that you would prefer that next time he ask you instead of assuming it is okay.
    c) Think about saying something to your neighbor but procrastinating because you want to keep the peace.

2. You are waiting in line to be seated at a restaurant and you notice that people who have come in later than you or who are behind you in line continue to get served while you continue to wait. How would you respond?

    a) Immediately go and sit down at the next available table, without being seated by the host.
    b) Speak to the host and point out that you have been waiting a long time and would like to be seated next.
    c) Say nothing in the hopes that you will be seated next.

3. You are camping with your family and in the site directly beside you there are noisy teenagers blaring music and using profanity. How would you respond?

    a) Blast your music louder than theirs and drown them out.
    b) Wait for the right opportunity to speak to one of them and tell them your concern about their behavior and that it will be reported to the park office if it happens again.
    c) Go to the park office and ask to move your campsite

4. Your boss asks you to stop by the printers to pick up materials for the office on your way to work because the print shop is close to your home. After a few times the boss cancels the delivery service and it just becomes a regular expectation that you will pick up all the boxes of printed materials. How would you respond?

    a) Tell your boss that you are being taken advantage of and file a grievance with the union.
    b) Tell your boss that you are able to help out once in a while but from now on you are going to be submitting an expense invoice for the mileage.
    c) Start taking the bus to work instead of driving.

The a) responses to these questions illustrate the aggressive approach to conflict; the c) responses represent passive approaches to dealing with conflict; and the b) responses represent an assertive response. To illustrate further, the conflict continuum can be depicted as is shown below, with assertiveness representing the balanced approach between the two extremes of passivity and aggression.

Passive | Asserive | Aggresive

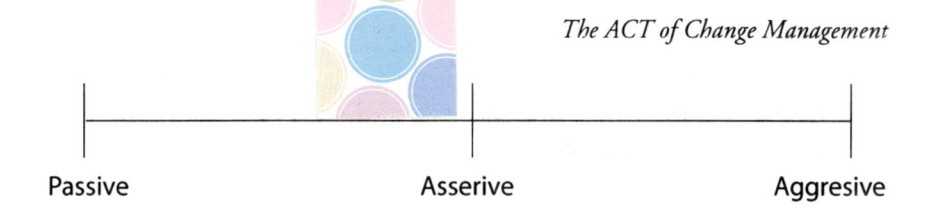

Assertive Language and Words

Most people in positions of leadership are very familiar with assertiveness and concepts such as "I assertion" and giving feedback. For this discussion it is not important to go into any great depth with these concepts, except to emphasize that both the passive response and the aggressive response represent extremes. Assertiveness represents a balanced response in which the individual is able to be direct in confronting conflict, communicating how they feel and working with the other party on problem solving.

How then does assertiveness come into play with ACT? It simply means that for the change leader, "their yes is their yes and their no is their no." There is no duplicity or doublespeak in what they communicate. "I assertion" is typically communicated through the agreement "if you do A then I will do B."

Example:

"Mary, if you continue to <u>come in late for work</u> (A) then I <u>will have to dock your pay</u> (B)."

You can even integrate feedback to create a more powerful impact. This involves not only pointing out the undesired behavior of the other but at the same time conveying how their behavior affects you and others; this should be followed by a proposed solution.

Example:

"When you do _____ I feel _____ because _____."

"Mary, when you continue to come into work late, it bothers me because it gives the impression that you do not have respect for your colleagues and the *organization. How can I work with you to improve and move towards creating a more positive workplace?"*

Notice that the second approach goes farther than the first by not only exposing the behaviour, but also ending constructively, with the change leader offering to help the employee change their own behaviour.

Assertive Body Language

Both "I assertion" and giving feedback are very effective techniques. Assertiveness not only means being assertive with language but also using assertiveness in non verbal communication and body language. Experts on this subject have stated that if there is inconsistency between the verbal and non-verbal communication of a message, it actually causes the receiver to go through an inner-conflict, as they are left with the impression that they are being deceived.

Now imagine the change leader confronting Mary for her lateness. The change leader says all the right words, but the leader's eyes are looking down (indicating shame or shyness); the leader is also using excessive hand gestures and speaking quickly and in a high pitch (indicating nervousness). If you were Mary, how would you take that feedback? The message was assertive, but the body language contradicted the message. If this were the case, it is likely that Mary would not take the change leader seriously at all and would continue to come in late.

Experts say that the perception of body language accounts for up to 90% of what people perceive in a message, while the actual words may only account for 10%. For a change leader to be perceived as assertive in their body language, here are some tips:

<u>Practice Slower Than Normal Movements</u>

This creates the perception of being in control. Powerful people who are in control are never rushed; they take their time.

Use Direct Eye Contact

In western cultures, direct eye contact usually conveys that one is focused and taking matters seriously. However, in eastern cultures direct eye contact may be intimidating.

Maintain A Serious But Professional Facial Expression

This is hard to describe without actually seeing it demonstrated. It means be focused and polite but not angry.

Be Aware Of Voice Tone

Use a low and commanding tone.

Be Aware Of The Rate And Flow Of Speech

Use a slow pace with occasional pauses.

Proper Stance

Standing with your shoulders pinned back, chest out and with your feet shoulder-length apart gives the appearance of being larger and confident.

Use Of Hand Gestures

In his book on giving presentations, Ron Hoff (1992) talks about the problems with nervous gestures. For many people, there is a need for tactile stimulus when they are feeling anxious. Hoff recommends letting your hands hang down to your sides comfortably. Touch forefinger to thumb with each hand for what he calls tactile reassurance.

Other Strategies: Visualization, Scripting, Rehearsal And Self-Talk

The best way for a change leader to employ these techniques is to actually rehearse or practice them. It may sound silly but it is good practice for the change leader; engaging in a kind of self-talk prepares them for the confrontation. It may mean going into their office, closing the door and visualizing what the confrontation might look like. Seeing and anticipating the encounter can actually help to reduce anxiety, particularly for those who struggle with confrontation.

The mindset of the change leader should be to approach confrontation by being direct and to deliver an emotionally balanced message to the employee. Most in this situation typically imagine the worst possible outcome and begin to play that scenario over and over in their minds, which only serves to further fuel their anxiety. To prevent this, the change leader can simply imagine how an employee might react and then write down some potential responses to each possible reaction. I call this technique "scripting." Scripting allows the change leader to pick a maximum of 3 talking points that absolutely need to be communicated to the employee and to practice how they would communicate them, as if reciting a script. It is best to avoid any long drawn-out speeches. More is less, meaning that some of the most powerful and assertive-seeming phrases actually say very little

Combining assertive language with assertive body language lends consistency to the change leader's message. This increases the leader's credibility with their employees and helps to eliminate employees' inner-conflicts and suspicion of deception from the change leader.

Assertiveness In Situations & Environment

Assertiveness can also apply to the way in which a change leader directly attends to specific situations. This means they do not wait or procrastinate; instead, they deal with problems expediently. We have all had experience with this in customer service settings. A typical scenario has the customer in a restaurant who complains that his or her meal is cold. An effective restaurant manager would not delay and would come directly to the table, address the issue, rectify the problem and perhaps even offer some side dish as compensation. However, many of us may have experienced the opposite situation, in which you cannot find a server and, when you do raise the problem, you end up waiting long periods before the issue is rectified, leaving you with a less than pleasant dining experience.

Attending to issues quickly gives the other party the perception that you are taking their concern seriously and that you value their feedback. Every change manager must also know when to use discretion and when to confront an issue or refrain from confronting an issue. I recall an experience I had with one of my supervisors who made me aware of a conflict between her and another employee who had a reputation for being negative. When I came over to speak to the supervisor and get more details, I noticed that the majority of employees in the area was close allies of the negative employee. Instead I changed my approach and decided to wait until the team leader was going on her break. I then walked out of the area with her and she was able to convey the details of the incident away from the others. Had I pulled the team leader aside at that moment to do fact finding, it would have made it obvious that we were talking about them. I am sure that afterward it would have made it a very difficult environment for the team leader. Although it is important to act on issues quickly it is equally important to use discretion if the change leader perceives that timing is critical to a successful outcome.

To summarize our discussion on assertiveness, it is clear that for the change leader, assertiveness includes three components:

1. Language and words
2. Body language
3. Situation and environment

Collaboration

"It doesn't take a hero to go into battle. It takes a hero to be one of those men who goes into battle." Gen. Norman Schwarzkopf

The second component of ACT includes the change leader being a team player. An effective team leader is willing to work alongside people to get the job done and leads according to these principles:

Focus On One To One Relationships

Vision is advanced one person at a time.

Putting The Needs Of Others First

The change leader must be selfless and put the needs of their employees before their own.

Building People Potential

The change leader must be able to assess each of their employee's talents and play to their strengths, not just their limitations.

Counseling Skills

A change leader wears many hats, one of which is the ability to provide support and direction to each individual employee when needed.

Shared Governance

An effective change leader shares power by delegating responsibility.

Daily Reflective Practice

E.g., what worked well today, what didn't work well today and what can I do better next time?

Being Solutions Focused

The ability to turn complaining into solutions.

Perhaps one of the best examples of collaborative leadership in history was British Prime Minister Winston Churchill. One of the reasons he was so revered by the military was because he was a solider himself who saw combat in his lifetime. This served to give him tremendous credibility and respect within the Armed Forces. It was even said that under the threat of bombs being dropped in London during World War II, he often gave speeches on the rooftops of buildings. He willingly put himself in harm's way, while other political leaders gave orders from safe places far from the theatres of war. Churchill and his wife were also known to walk openly down the streets of London shortly after bombs had been dropped and they even went so far as to have their own food rationed just like the rest of the people of Britain, when they clearly did not need to. These types of acts demonstrated solidarity with the people of Britain and won their leader their respect and trust.

Although every change leader must keep professional distance and avoid becoming a peer of their employees, it is also important that they not be afraid to roll up their sleeves and work alongside their employees when the occasion requires it. This can only serve to build up a change leader's credibility.

Transparency

Transparency means:

- You say what you mean and mean what you say.

- You have no hidden agenda.

- People always know what to expect from you.

- You make it clear what you expect from others.

When I began my career as a manager I had to come up with a quick way to connect with my employees. So, I developed the acronym ACT to make it clear that this is what they can expect from me and what I would expect from them. I used ACT to orientate every new employee that I hire. With a new hire, I would be honest with them and tell them that they were going to encounter some great employees who they could learn a great deal from, as well as some not so great and negative employees who they would need to be careful around. However, I would never mention the specific names of any negative employees because the new hire would eventually discover them. Sure enough, in one case they did. After I gave a new hire that speech, in a few hours she was back in my office, saying "you were right. The minute I walked into the employee's room I could hear the bitter complaining." My advice to those new hires was that when they heard complaining they should extricate themselves and have no part of it, because the longer they sat and listened the more likely it was that they would end up succumbing to the peer pressure and become negative as well.

One of the biggest complaints that employees have against management in any organization is the accusation that management has a "hidden agenda." Early in my career I fell into this trap when I was a frontline worker. I was young and very impressionable and I made the mistake of aligning myself with some disgruntled employees. I soon found myself sucked into believing that management were a diabolical group of masterminds who sat around a boardroom table plotting how they could manipulate and exploit the employees next. In reality, nothing could have been further from the truth. In actuality, most in management make decisions pragmatically, and rarely with the malevolence that frontline workers often can be led to believe.

When I got into management, I was astounded at some of the rumors that would circulate around the organization. I realized that the further one went up the ladder of leadership, the wider their perspective becomes in regard to the way in which decisions have to be made. That also means that those at the front lines typically hear fragments of information and then draw conclusions based on a fixed belief that "management is out to screw us." One of the best examples of this that I have heard of was about an organization that was planning to roll out a new performance appraisal program. One of the union stewards went around claiming that management were profiling people.

To try to dispel the rumor mill, I would tell my employees that, if they had any questions or concerns, to bring them directly to me. If I could answer the question I would. If I was not able to answer, for confidentiality reasons, then I would tell them that too. If I did not know the answer, I would try my best to find out. I observed that most employees would stop to ask me questions; however, no matter how much I reinforced that I was transparent, the negative employees continued to refuse to ask me things.

I realized that this was deliberate. If they asked me a question based on their "management is out to screw us" template, and the answer I gave contradicted that template, then they would have nothing to complain and gossip about.

Fundamental Attribution Bias

Fundamental Attribution Bias refers to the fact that when it comes to explaining our own behavior, we are most likely to attribute it to an external cause. However, when it comes to explaining the undesirable behavior of others, we are more likely to attribute it to an internal cause, meaning we make a value judgment of that person's character. To use the example of road rage, if you are driving and someone cuts you off, your first reaction is to get angry and call the person an idiot, with the assumption being that they did the act on purpose. However, let's suppose instead that I witnessed you cutting someone off in traffic and then asked you why you did it. You probably would say that it was an accident, perhaps because you were about to miss your turn and forgot to check your blind spot. To apply that to a workplace setting, I have observed that the most negative people do not see themselves as negative.

This is important for a change leader to understand. Most employees do not get up in the morning with the plan to go into work and make everyone's life miserable. Most negative employees are responding to a years of self-conditioning based on Fundamental Attribution Bias.

Consider the employee who takes longer than normal breaks or disappears for long periods of time without authorization. One could consider their behavior a "theft of time" that warrants discipline. However, that employee might think to themselves that they have been in the organization for 25 years, and that they are underpaid and exploited by management anyway, so their behavior is justified. They rationalize to themselves that management owes them. Again, the template that says "management is out to screw employees" is applied to almost any setting. Let's take this a step further and suppose that one day, just to be nice, you come to work with coffee and donuts for everyone. Most of the employees will say thank you. However, the negative employees are probably thinking: "why is he doing this?" or "what is his ulterior motive?" You simply wanted to raise morale and provide a kind gesture but the template comes into play again, despite your best intentions. There truly is no remedy for this, but the change leader must be aware of it and anticipate it, all while avoiding letting it discourage them from doing what they know is right.

ACT Expanded Beyond The Workplace

At one workshop I did on ACT, one of the evaluations had an interesting comment. The participant wrote, "I am going to use ACT all the time in my personal life too."

When I developed ACT, I found that once I started integrating ACT at work it ended up becoming a way of living. I started integrating it into my interpersonal relationships as well. The more I practiced being assertive, collaborative and transparent at work, the more confident I became when I was interacting with people in my personal life.

I also found that when I was in public, at a restaurant or bank, I would find myself using ACT more and more, particularly in situations of conflict, in which I would normally back down for the sake of keeping the peace or because I felt it just wasn't worth it to resolve the issue at hand. ACT is a principled approach and is not intended for self-justification. Actually, it is quite the opposite. ACT is not about standing up for yourself as much as it is about standing up for what is right.

I began to wonder what would happen if people in general were more assertive, collaborative and transparent all the time and with everyone? Think about how much conflict would be avoided. Especially consider how productive and happier we might be in the workplace if people tactfully said what was on their minds in a spirit of problem solving and without bias or suspicion of ulterior motive.

Persevering Through Adversity

In an article published in the Harvard Business Review, Warren Bennis and Robert Thomas (2002) use the term "crucibles" to help leaders change their perspective by viewing crises as events that help to define them as leaders, as opposed to events that could destroy them.

Bennis and Thomas go on to state that a leader can find meaning in negative events and learn from even the most difficult of circumstances. When the name Rudolph Giuliani is raised, what immediately comes to your mind? The answer is obvious: New York City, September 11, 2001. People vividly remember the images of him walking down lower Manhattan as the planes struck the twin towers, with rubble and smoke filing the streets and people scrambling in terror. What he is remembered for most is his leadership during the crisis and his compassion towards New Yorkers as he tried to round people up and lead them to safety. In one of his most famous statements during this period Giuliani said:

"Tomorrow New York is going to be here. And we're going to rebuild, and we're going to be stronger than we were before . . . . I want the people of New York to be an example to the rest of the country, and the rest of the world, that terrorism can't stop us."

(Giuliani, 2001)

Giuliani's career prior to that it was also marked with significant achievements. In the 1970's and 1980's, New York City was in tremendous debt. Many businesses began to move out of the city due to the high taxes and a high crime rate that included mafia activity. Giuliani turned the economy of New York around and made it lucrative for businesses to move back to the city. When he was a district attorney, he convicted the heads of eleven mafia crime families, as well as numerous white collar criminals on Wall Street. From 1994 to 2002, the rate of major crimes in the New York area dropped dramatically. Although Giuliani was unsuccessful in his presidential campaign for various reasons his management of 9/11 distinguished him as an exceptional leader. According to Bennis and Thomas, leaders need to build the skills required to overcome adversity and to come out of a crisis stronger than they were before.

Transcendence

For the change leader who feels trapped by crisis, the challenge is to step back from adversity and get a big picture view of things. Adversity can help the change leader discover meaning and principles, and to learn from challenges. A change leader who is able to endure adversity will come out far stronger than they were before. Crucibles specifically refer to a trial or test. These times in the wilderness are often the loneliest for the change leader. However, in times of solitude there is an opportunity to engage in deep self-reflection. Crisis will force the change leader to discover who they are and what they are made of, as well as challenge their own values and principles. Crisis and hardship also serve to make a change leader's focus clearer and help them to fine-tune their judgment. It also serves to help them develop a "thicker skin" when it comes to the ability to absorb criticism and not allow it to derail their leadership. Somehow, change leaders who survive the wilderness emerge with a changed identity. Adversity will make you either better or bitter.

To use an illustration from nature, few people are aware that an eagle can actually fly above a storm. It senses the storms before it hits, then takes off and lets the winds of the storm push it higher and higher until it is able to soar above the storm. Applied to the change leader, this suggests that the change leader must be sensitive and alert to an upcoming crisis and then allow the pressures to push them higher, to transcend the crisis. Transcending in this sense means remaining above the problem and keeping a big picture perspective on it, as opposed to being "in the problem," where options appear more limited than they really are.

For many great leaders, adversity can actually be a launching pad for an opportunity to define their leadership. If you can bear up under adversity and brave a challenge, you will win the respect of the people around you. In the experience of one change leader, she found that her employees were always watching her to see how she would react and handle tough situations; they wanted to know whether or not she would crack under pressure. She came into work early one morning to find a very angry and belligerent employee using profanity and putting down another team member, who was not there. The other employees sat silent as she continued her tirade, but then looked at the change leader as if to ask "what are you going to do about this?" She calmly walked up to the angry employee, took her by the arm and said "come with me please." Then, she escorted the angry employee into another room where the change leader firmly admonished her and warned her about her behavior. The other employees could not hear what the change leader was saying but they were able to see that this employee was going to be held accountable for her behavior and that her unprofessional conduct would not be tolerated. This was ACT in action:

> *Assertive*, in this instance, meant dealing with the issue immediately and directly, before the situation escalated.
>
> *Collaborative* meant that in the discussion the change leader also found an opportunity to value her for her experience and leadership, and to challenge her to be a positive leader and not to demoralize her team by cutting others down.
>
> *Transparent* meant that she made her expectation very clear: from now on, the employee would conduct herself with professionalism, and if she had a problem with her colleague she would go and speak to the leader directly. If the behavior continued it would be met with consequences.

The change leader must always be cognizant that people are watching how they react to certain situations. Negative employees will often test leaders to see how far they can push them and whether or not they will crack under the pressure. Change leaders must always remain in control in a crisis and never allow themselves to be rattled. A speaker I once heard talked about the fact that everyone has a "hot button," something that really gets under their skin and gets a reaction. Negative employees will seek the hot button of the change leader and continually push it to get that reaction. Recall the template of "management is out to get us." Any harsh reaction from the change leader will only seek to reinforce that perception.

Most people have had the unfortunate experience of working under a tyrannical boss or manager. If we were to ask that dictatorial boss where he or she learned to manage people this leader would probably say that they were once treated that way by their superiors. Just as with negative employees who don't see themselves as negative, the same holds true for negative managers. They feel that they need to break people down and manipulate them through fear and coercion. Unfortunately, fear and coercion gets results in the short term, but in the long term these tactics do not pay off.

To illustrate, I remember watching a football game in which the coach (famous for being very drill sergeant-like) started chewing out his players on the sidelines for their poor performance, in addition to berating them publically during his press conferences. In a televised game, cameras zoomed in on the coach screaming at the quarterback, who had just thrown an interception. What stuck with me was not the coach verbally berating the player, but look on the players face. He looked like a teenager staring off into space, rolling his eyes at his father, who was yelling at him for bringing the car home late. In other words, he was tuning the coach out.

Unfortunately for the dictatorial-tyrant leader, this is what will ultimately happen. After a while, the threats and coercion will no longer intimidate anyone and people will just get fed up and not take him or her seriously anymore. So the question is asked: "why then does the dictatorial-tyrant use such tactics in the first place?" The answer is that they do this because they do not know how to motivate people. An effective change leader does not need to use the tactics of the dictator-tyrant because he or she knows techniques that positively motivate and persuade their employees. Motivation and persuasion aimed at creating change will be covered in more depth in a later chapter.

ACT & The Change Continuum

People are at different stages of readiness when it comes to change. The diagram below illustrates this better:

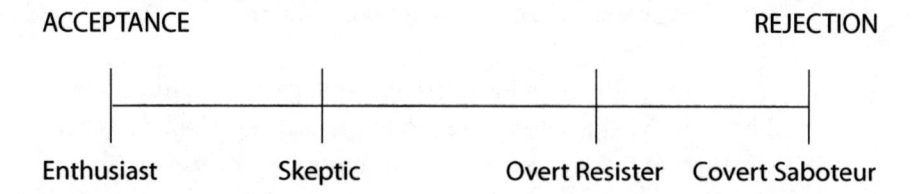

ACCEPTANCE   REJECTION

Enthusiast   Skeptic   Overt Resister   Covert Saboteur

The *enthusiast* is the person who is most likely to accept change. These are the people that the change leader must invest in the most, because they have the ability to positively influence others with their energy and positive behavior.

The *skeptic* is the one who is open to change but needs more convincing. The change leader must find opportunities to work with that individual by presenting evidence and working towards persuading them to accept the change.

The *overt resister* is the one who either remains silent when presented with new ideas or openly refuses to cooperate. The change leader needs to be diligent and aware that this individual can negatively influence others and be prepared to take them to task if they are insubordinate.

The *covert resister* is the one who is perhaps the most dangerous. They openly act as if they are in agreement with the changes but the moment the change leader turns their back they will actively sabotage. Covert resisters are typically passive aggressive and the best means of dealing with them is to actually call them out and expose them.

Below are some scenarios to consider, in which ACT can be applied to organizational change:

<u>Enthusiast</u>

- *Assertive*—be direct with the information that you are happy they are on board. Tell them you intend to invest resources to grow and develop them further.

- *Collaborative*—involve them in planning committees.

- *Transparent*—ask them for feedback and allow them to hold you accountable for being consistent with the organization's mission, vision and values.

<u>Skeptic</u>

- *Assertive*—tell them that you sense that they are not convinced and that you value them enough to find ways to help them understand and appreciate the new vision.

- *Collaborative*—ask them what they would need to convince them, and schedule future coaching sessions in which you can openly dialogue and address their concerns. Also, be prepared to use their talents as trouble shooters in a quality-control role. It may be that their concerns are legitimate and can be addressed constructively.

- *Transparent*—be honest and tell them that it is okay for them to disagree but that you will expect them to "vent up" and channel their concerns to you directly, instead of outwardly to their peers, where it might serve to demoralize the team.

Overt Resister

- *Assertive*—go directly to them when you observe blatant insubordination and address it on the spot to prevent them from doing more damage and to make an example in front of others that you mean business.

- *Collaborative*—take them to task in regard to the impact of their behavior on the organization and your expectations as to proper conduct; offer supports and even educational opportunities to help them.

- *Transparent*—if necessary, let them know that the next occurrence will escalate to formal discipline, if warranted.

Covert Saboteur

- *Assertive*—Find the right time to get them one on one and take them to task because you have noticed that they are saying one thing but actively doing another in order to undermine your authority and the new vision.

- *Collaborative*—provide specific examples of their behavior and do some coaching as to how a situation could have been handled better.

- *Transparent* - if necessary, let them know that the next occurrence will escalate to formal discipline, if warranted.

Review Of Key Principles

Before the change leader tries to change others he or she must first integrate ACT into themselves, both personally and professionally.

Assertiveness involves three parts: assertive language, assertive body language and assertiveness in situations.

Collaboration involves the change leader working alongside their employees and demonstrating solidarity.

Transparency means the change leader must anticipate and be aware of factors such as fundamental attribution bias when it comes to how the employees perceive the behavior of the change leader.

Adversity works to refine leadership skills and to define a change leader.

The change leader must assess where their employees fall on the change continuum and use ACT to help them respond appropriately in order to advance their vision.

CHAPTER 4

EMPLOYEE ACHIEVEMENT & APTITUDE

A key component of the ACT model involves the change leader assessing each employee's performance. To do so involves two critical areas: achievement and aptitude.

Achievement refers to each employee's level of productivity in the organization. As we will see, not all employees achieve at the same level. Naturally, some achieve what is expected of them, some exceed expectations and some underachieve. Aptitude refers to their potential to succeed in the organization. Some of this is due to motivation and some to natural abilities and talents. When we place both achievement and aptitude on an X and Y axis, it gives us four quadrants. For a more complete concept of this, see the description and illustration below:

High achievement and low aptitude = Status Quo

High achievement and high aptitude = Change Agents

Low achievement and high aptitude = Instigators

Low achievement and low aptitude = Burnouts

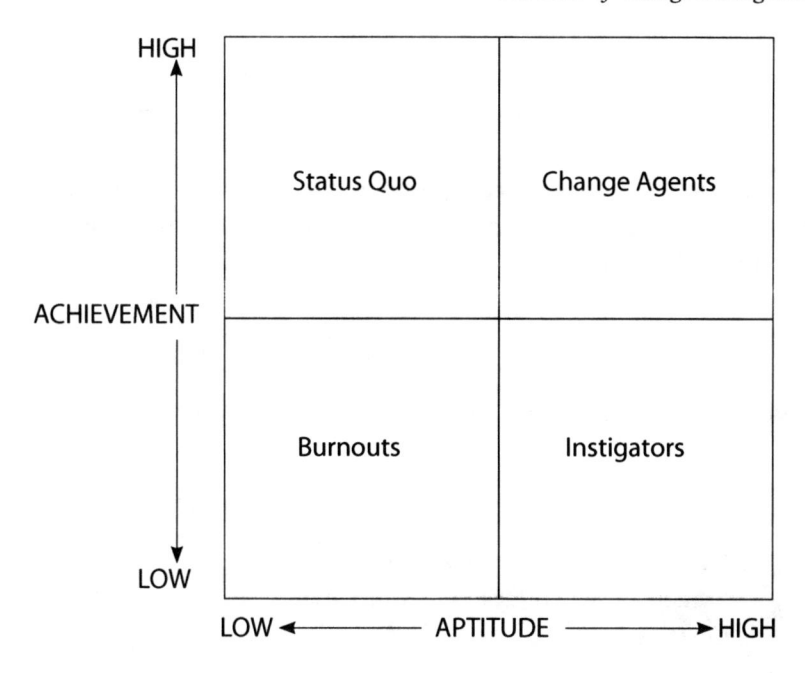

```
                    HIGH
                     ▲
                     |
                     |  ┌─────────────────┬─────────────────┐
                     |  │                 │                 │
                     |  │                 │                 │
                     |  │   Status Quo    │  Change Agents  │
                     |  │                 │                 │
                     |  │                 │                 │
    ACHIEVEMENT      |  ├─────────────────┼─────────────────┤
                     |  │                 │                 │
                     |  │                 │                 │
                     |  │    Burnouts     │   Instigators   │
                     |  │                 │                 │
                     |  │                 │                 │
                     ▼  └─────────────────┴─────────────────┘
                    LOW
                        LOW ◄─────── APTITUDE ───────► HIGH
```

To have an effective organization you need to employ a 3-pronged strategy:

1. Empower Your Change Agents

These individuals are catalysts for change. They are natural leaders and are critical to the success of any change initiative.

2. Recognize Your Status Quo Employees

These individuals hold up the organization and if you neglect them things fall apart. These individuals typically sit on the fence. They are the key group and they need to be positively influenced and persuaded.

3. Performance Manage Your Instigators and Burnouts

Left unchecked, these individuals do tremendous damage. The change leader must identify them early on and begin the process of holding them accountable and forcing them into making a choice. This is covered in more depth in chapter eight.

We will now examine each category of employees, what motivates them and the possible positive and negative outcomes of which the change leader must be aware.

Change Agent

(High Achievement/High Aptitude)

Characteristics that describe this group include:

- Positive attitude towards work
- Exceeds productivity and performance
- Creative
- Flexible
- Consistent
- Natural leader
- Requires little supervision
- Exceptional - doesn't mean they are better than others, it means they are more effective in a given area.

Motivated by: Opportunity

Change agents have the ability to inspire confidence in themselves and others. They are sincere, genuine and have integrity of character. They naturally take charge of situations and people will follow their lead. They are also able to sense leadership in others, can motivate and can communicate the right messages to get the team moving. Change agents are also passionate about what they do because they have gifts and skills in areas in which most people do not. They generate an excitement that is contagious. They love to experiment and to create new ways of doing things.

Long term:

(+) They will help to positively influence an organization.

Rachel was a fairly new hire with just about a year under her belt. Soon after she started she demonstrated an excellence in her duties. She came to work very positive and upbeat. Even when there was negativity around her she remained true to her principles and values, maintaining excellent client service. She was given an opportunity by her change leader to become a project leader. Her leadership grew and matured even more from this experience.

(-) They will become an instigator or leave.

Nora was hired into the organization as a seasoned veteran with years of experience. She impressed everyone with her credentials as well as her natural leadership and assertiveness. When she started she did not back down from negativity and often called people out on their poor conduct. She was instrumental in refining and streamlining the operation. However, the toxicity in the organization eventually began to put a strain on Nora. She was soon ostracized and became the subject of harassment and bullying. Despite all attempts to support her, she found it increasingly difficult to stand alone against the negative employees. Eventually she began to identify with the negative employees and decided that it was easier to join them than to fight them. The tragedy of the story is that Nora ended up conspiring to sabotage the change leader. The relationship soured and she eventually transferred away, angry and bitter.

Status Quo

(High Achievement / Low Aptitude)

Characteristics that describe this group include:

- Dependable
- Reliable
- Steady
- Works hard and produces consistent results

- In most organizations, these are the people we tend to neglect because the problem children get all the attention.

- Often are taken for granted

- Appear to have low potential, but is it actually untapped potential?

Motivated by: Recognition

Research has proven that the leading cause of employees leaving an organization is not financial but, rather, is related to a lack of recognition. Recognition=retention; we will cover this in more depth in chapter seven.

Long term:

(+) They may develop into a change agent

The change leader must decide whether or not this employee truly has no aptitude. It is more likely that they have potential that is untapped or undiscovered. The goal of the change agent is to discover that individual's talents and abilities. In one instance, there was a new employee who started in an organization and who was just out of school and very green. Many of his colleagues began to complain about his shy and complacent demeanor, as well as his failure to be self-directed in his work. However, when the organization moved to a new computerized system, this employee volunteered for a train the trainer program, where he excelled. It turned out that his talent was in the use of technology. When the program was rolled out, he went around the department as a mentor, teaching and training others. As his confidence level was elevated, so was his overall performance. His demeanor changed and he was more relaxed, personable with his peers and his productivity also increased. In fact many of his peers who were older and less computer literate expressed their appreciation of his assistance in helping them learn the new system.

(-) They will burn out or leave

It is very intriguing to examine the parallels between parenting and managing in several contexts. To illustrate, think of a family situation with one child who is responsible and another who is a rule-breaker. Who do the parents ultimately pay more attention to? The problem child. Inadvertently, they will neglect the responsible child to the point where the responsible child has to act out to get attention. The responsible child feels that even though they behave themselves, they do not get the same attention as their sibling who acts out. What happens when the steady child who behaves gets neglected? They end up becoming resentful. The same can be said of the employee in this category. If they feel that they are giving all they can and it is going unnoticed, they may eventually seek employment elsewhere. Or even worse, they may remain but become disgruntled and become an instigator, or even a burnout, causing negativity in the organization and impeding progress and change.

Instigator

(Low Achievement/ High Aptitude)

Characteristics that describe this group include:

- Troublemakers

- Negative leaders

- Passive aggressive

- Under-stimulated

- Under productive

- Engages in splitting, i.e. dividing the employees and turning people on each other

Motivated by: Challenge & Power

Long term:

(+) They can develop into a change agent.

Charles was a veteran who showed flashes of potential but had a negative attitude the majority of the time. His peers complained that he was lazy and did not do his share of work. He also frequently complained about the organization to his peers and wrote negative emails to the change leader, venting his frustrations. Upon analysis, his work environment was found to be toxic and he was clearly being dragged down by the poor behavior of his peers. However, when the work culture shifted and became positive, he actually began to step up. The change leader discovered that Charles had untapped potential. He was an excellent trouble shooter and the change leader found a way to channel his complaining into something productive. Charles would often complain about equipment problems, so the change leader gave him a job doing inventory and producing a report and making recommendations. Not only did Charles do the report, he also brought in his tool box and spent time actually fixing the equipment. From that point on, he began expressing creative ideas and became far more productive in his work.

(-) They will continue to disrupt if left unaccountable and unchallenged.

Dena was well liked by clients because she did her job really well. She was reliable and consistent in her work. She was a 25 year veteran who felt threatened by the new changes brought in by the organization. She responded to the changes by sabotaging the change leader. She would say all the right things when the change leader was around, but behind the scenes she was assassinating her character and forcing employees to choose sides. The change leader began to build a case of insubordination and misconduct against Dena. However, when she presented the case to her superiors it was met with complacency and no commitment to hold her accountable. The longer the organization refused to deal with Dena, the more damage she caused. The organization underwent a very large employee turnover in a one year period, due mostly to the behavior of Dena.

Burnouts

(Low Achievement / Low Aptitude)

Characteristics that describe this group include:

- Under-productive

- Rigid

- Task-focused

- Does the bare minimum

- Lazy

- Un-teachable

Motivated by: Money

Long term:

(+) They can become reliable

Arlene's colleagues complained about her constantly. She frequently made mistakes in her duties and others ended up having to do her work as well as their own. When the change leader would confront Arlene, she would typically become defensive; she blamed others and refused to take responsibility for her own actions. Eventually Arlene's poor performance jeopardized her employment. The change leader made one last attempt to reach Arlene and was candid about the fact that she was on the brink of termination. Every time Arlene tried to displace the blame onto others the change leader refused to hear it and continually threw it back to Arlene and pushed her to make a decision. Eventually Arlene conceded and agreed to be put on a remediation plan. A year later, the complaints from her colleagues stopped and she moved up to being a reliable employee, as her performance improved from poor to satisfactory, which was a realistic goal for her to aim at.

(-) They will continue to take up space and/or quit eventually.

Bonnie had a reputation as a burn out. She simply did not care about her colleagues or clients. Her attitude was extremely negative and her performance was beyond substandard. Previous change leaders were afraid of her due to her angry and intimidating demeanor. She was a bully who would target and ruin any employee who opposed her. Finally, another change leader came along who was not afraid of Bonnie. She was direct with Bonnie and would confront her immediately about her conduct and performance. After a while, her file became thicker with counseling letters, warning letters and more progressive discipline. While this occurred, the team culture began to change and the team was becoming more positive and progressive. Bonnie's previous actions were deemed unacceptable to her peers, who became frustrated with her constant negativity. In the end, Bonnie lost her influence and transferred out of that department to another.

Assessing Attitude & Achievement Using 80/20 & Critical Mass

Recall from the discussion in Chapter 2 regarding the Pareto principle, which states that there is an imbalance between inputs and outputs. Input is not usually equal to output. Instead, 80% of productivity results from 20% of effort. A change agent who understands Pareto will also know that investing in the correct 20% of people will yield an 80% change. Recall also from Chapter 2 Gladwell's principle of "The Tipping Point," which states that change occurs when a given variable reaches 20% mass. When combined, these two principles create a very powerful strategy for change. Before we discover what that strategy is, let us first examine the way in which we can practically assess the employees in our organization.

Worksheet #1

Instructions

On the chart, analyze the employees that you are responsible for overseeing, or who you are in a position to influence. Determine the category you would place them, according to achievement vs. aptitude (e.g., Change Agent, Status Quo, Instigators and Burnouts). Note: If you are not sure and feel that an employee belongs in more than one category, then make your best guess considering which category defines them the most.

Enter their initials in the appropriate category and then count up the number of employees in each category. Remember to indicate the total number of employees at the bottom of the chart.

The ACT of Change Management

Worksheet #1

Category	Initials Of Employees	Number Of Employees
+ (Change Agents)		
+\- (Status Quo)		
- (Instigators, Burnouts)		
	Total Number N =	

Analysis:

What do you notice? Which category has the most number of employees? Which has the least? Is there an imbalance? Proceed now to Worksheet #2 using the same data.

Worksheet #2

Instructions

For N at the top of the vertical axis, indicate the total number of employees that you are responsible for overseeing or that you are in a position to influence. Then create a scale on the vertical axis. The line halfway between N and 0 would represent 50%, meaning that half the employee would fall below it and half would fall above that line.

For example: If N=20, then the halfway line would be 10.

Using the data from Worksheet #1, plot your data points according to how many fall in each percentile.

Draw a line to connect all points.

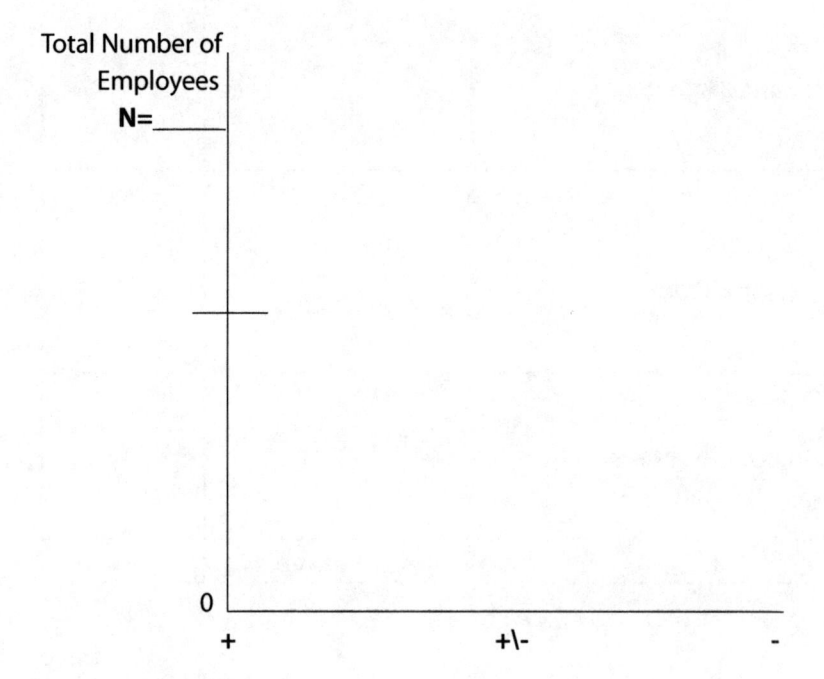

```
Total Number of
   Employees
      N=_____
        |
        |
        |
        |
        |
        |—
        |
        |
        |
        |
       0|_____
        +              +\-              -
```

Graphing Analysis

Now compare your graph to the ones below and determine which one most closely resembles your assessment of your employees.

A)   Bell Curve: Example Of An Average Organization

In most typical organizations, the graph resembles something like a bell curve. Inevitably, the +\- 60 or "Status Quo," account for the largest group in the organization. See below:

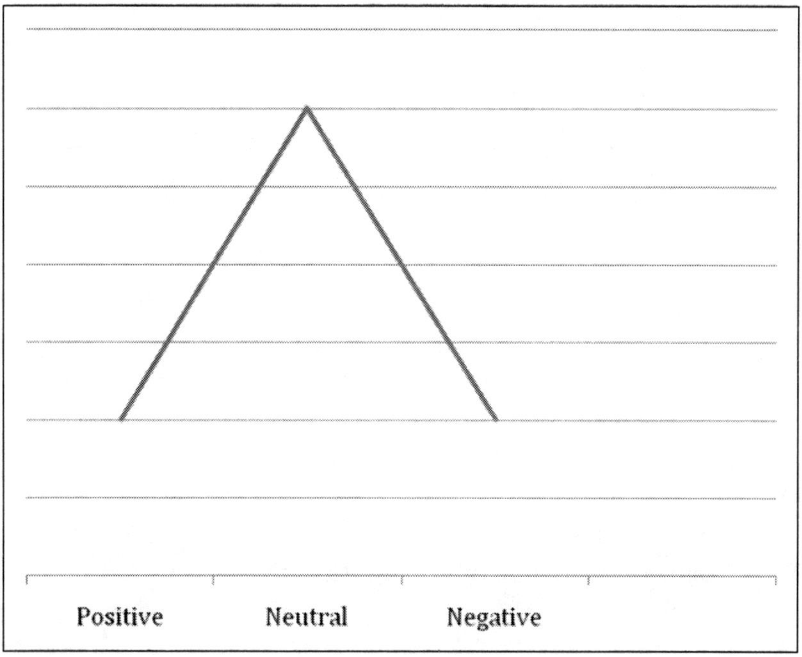

In the average organization, the distribution typically looks something like this:

+ 20% Positive "Change Agents"

+\- 60% Neutral "Status Quo"

- 20% Negative "Instigators and Burn outs"

B) Level line: Example Of An Organization In Transition

In this example, all three categories are virtually equal. This typically represents an organization that is going through some type of transition or change. Employees are either moving up or down, but all are experiencing some level of uncertainly and anxiety about the future.

```
|                                              |
|----------------------------------------------|
|  ▄▄▄▄▄▄▄▄▄▄▄▄▄▄▄▄▄▄▄▄▄                       |
|                                              |
|                                              |
|                                              |
|                                              |
|                                              |
|    Positive      Neutral      Negative       |
```

In the transitioning organization, the distribution typically looks something like this:

+ 33% Positive "Change Agents"

+\- 33% Neutral "Status Quo"

- 33% Negative "Instigators and Burn outs"

C)   Negative Skew: Example Of Culture Of Entitlement

In this organization, the number of negative employees outweighs the number of positive employees, creating a negative skew. In this example, the negative employees are influencing the neutral majority. When you combine the negative and neutral they may create as high as a—80% downward shift towards a culture of entitlement (chapter five will examine in more detail this type of organizational culture). In most cases, the truly negative employees make up only a handful of people, but their scope of influence is profound. Left unaddressed, the + 20% of positive employee will quickly burn themselves out trying to survive in a toxic workplace, or they will leave the organization altogether.

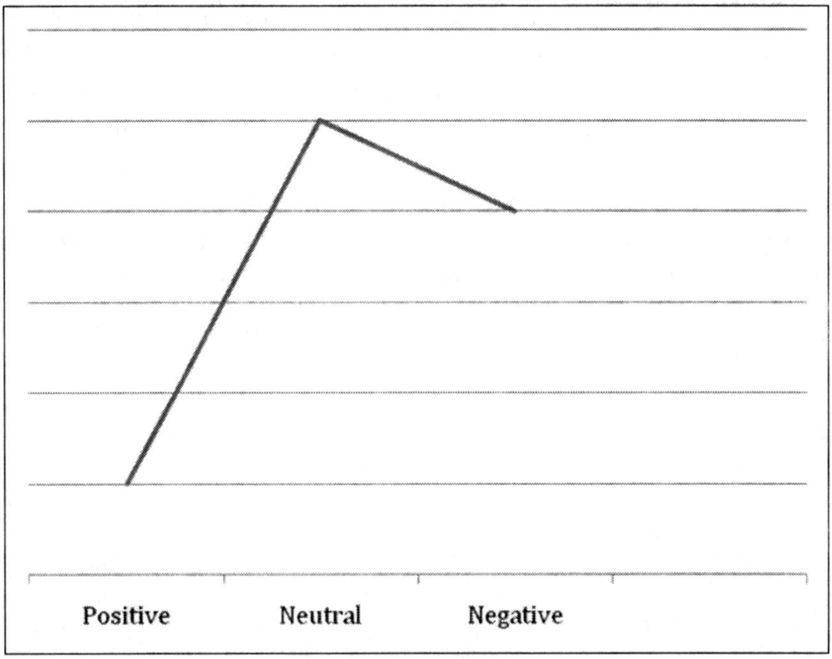

In the Negative Culture of Entitlement, the distribution typically looks something like this:

+ 20% Positive "Change Agents"

- 80% (composed of +\- 60% Neutral "Status Quo" plus 20% Negative "Instigators and Burn outs")

Notice that in this culture there appears to be only 2 groups, positive and negative, which means the organization is polarized and employees are being forced to take sides. In the process of change, the change leader will ultimately separate the neutral from the negative and create 3 groups, restoring balance towards influencing a positive skew, or a Culture of Achievement.

D) Positive Skew: Example Of Culture Of Achievement

In this organization the culture has shifted significantly towards the positive. Now the employees are polarized again but in a better sense; + 80% are positive comprised of + 20% change agents plus +\- Status Quo. This is due to the change agents having a positive influence on the neutral majority. This culture is marked by employees benchmarking with achievement rather than complaining. Employees are empowered and productive. The change leader is not spending as much time and energy trying to performance manage the remaining—20%. Instead, he or she is investing their time into delegating responsibility and maximizing operational performance.

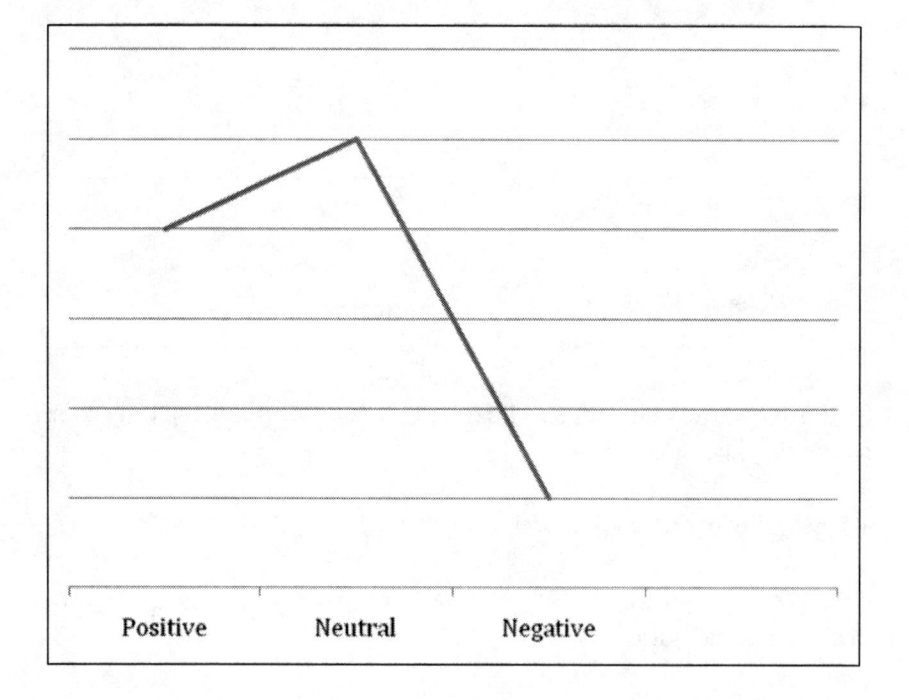

In the Positive Culture of Achievement, the distribution typically looks something like this:

+ 80% (composed of + 20% Positive "Change Agents" plus +\- 60% Neutral "Status Quo")

- 20%. Negative. "Instigators and Burnouts" are now isolated and exposed for the change leader to begin the process of performance management.

Your Analysis

Use five adjectives to describe the culture among the employees you lead; e.g. angry, productive, whining, caring, positive, etc.

1._____

2._____

3._____

4._____

5._____

Now, look at the line graph and indicate which of the following resembles the line you plotted.

   a) Bell curve
   b) Level line
   c) Negative skew
   d) Positive skew

Do you see a correlation between the culture in your organization and your graphing assessment? What does this mean for you as the change leader in terms of a starting point towards positive change?

If your graph closest resembles the bell curve, then you have an advantage in that there is balance in your organization. However, balance often signifies status quo. Being a truly effective change leader means taking the risk of positively polarizing your employee towards a positive skew or a culture of achievement.

If your graph is level, then it may indicate that some type of change is already occurring, either within or beyond your control. What is required here is for the change leader to be aware of it and to begin guiding it towards positive change. Left unattended, the line will naturally skew to the negative. Why? Because negativity spreads easier than positivity. All it takes is one person to become bitter. Anger, complaining and the victim mentality are the natural order of things in the workplace. To illustrate, just stand in line with a group of strangers for some type of entertainment or sporting event. Initially, everyone is positive, upbeat, excited and talking about their anticipation of having a good experience. Now let's say for the sake of argument that the event is delayed 15 minutes, then 30 minutes, then an hour. Very quickly the positive anticipation will turn to grumbling. If no one knows the cause of the delay, then the crowd will make assumptions, which will automatically be negative. Those assumptions will involve assigning blame, and so it goes. The change leader in the transitional organization must carefully monitor events and make all efforts to keep their employees informed as to what changes are occurring and why, in addition to actively working towards a shift to a more positive culture.

Traditional Thinking

Consider the average organization:

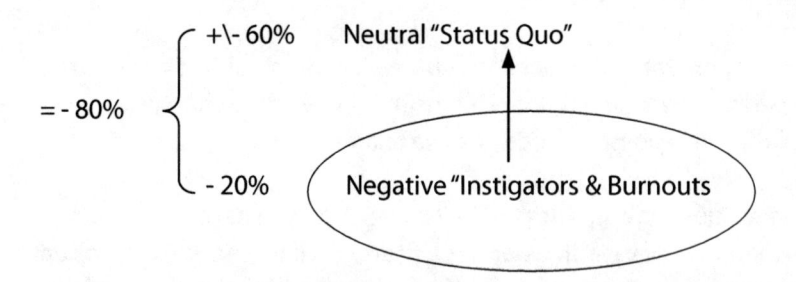

+ 20%   Positive Change Agents

= - 80% { +\- 60%   Neutral "Status Quo"

         - 20%   Negative "Instigators & Burnouts"

When the negative 20% have a strong influence, they will exert their influence and negatively influence the neutral 60%, creating a negative 80% majority. The result will be a culture of entitlement and a toxic workplace. Any change proposed in this context will be sabotaged and any potential change agent will no doubt become a target for attack. The biggest mistake that a change leader can make in this scenario is to focus all their energy on performance managing the negative 20%; to do so ignores the positive 20%, who are the ultimate cause of change.

Changing Mindset

However, if we take the same average organization and change our strategy by empowering the positive 20%, then through positive leadership they will ultimately influence the neutral 60%. When both groups are added together, the result is an 80% positive shift towards a culture of achievement. The remaining negative 20% become exposed and can then be methodically performance managed. See the chart below.

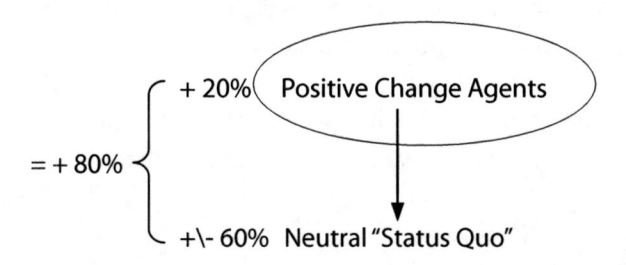

$$= +80% \begin{cases} +20\% & \text{Positive Change Agents} \\ \\ +\backslash- 60\% & \text{Neutral "Status Quo"} \end{cases}$$

$$-20\% \quad \text{Negative "Instigators \& Burnouts}$$

Review Of Key Principles

To have an effective organization, the change leader must assess employee aptitude and achievement and influence those measures using a 3-pronged strategy:

    1.   <u>Recognize The Status Quo</u> (covered in more detail in chapter 6)

    These individuals hold up the organization; if we neglect them things fall apart. These individuals typically sit on the fence. They are the key group that needs to be positively influenced and persuaded.

2. <u>Empower The Change Agents</u> (covered in more detail in chapter 7)

These individuals are catalysts for change. They are natural leaders and are critical to the success of any change initiative.

3. <u>Performance Manage The Instigators and Burnouts</u> (covered in more detail in chapter 9)

Left unchecked, these individuals do tremendous damage. The change leader must identify them and begin the process of holding them accountable and forcing them to make a choice.

Chapter 9 will present case studies that will provide tangible examples of the ways in which this strategy can be used to spur successful organizational change.

CHAPTER 5

Assessing Organizational Culture & Influencing Behavior Change

Workplace Culture Assessment

Rate your organization based on which statement best describes your culture:

1	Completely disagree
2	Disagree somewhat
3	Neutral or average
4	Mostly agree
5	Completely agree

Employees feel that they owe the client the best care or service that they can provide.

1		2		3		4		5

Employees show a keen interest in upgrading their skills through education.

1		2		3		4		5

Employees are progressive and forward thinking.

1		2		3		4		5

Employees are intrinsically motivated (i.e. self-motivated, not externally motivated or for money).

1   2   3   4   5

There is a high level of trust among the team members and towards management.

1   2   3   4   5

There is a high level of respect among team members and towards management.

1   2   3   4   5

There is positive cohesion amongst team members.

1   2   3   4   5

Employees are willing to take positive risks.

1   2   3   4   5

Employees hold each other accountable for their performance and conduct.

1   2   3   4   5

Employees are teachable and open to new ideas and new ways of doing things.

1   2   3   4   5

Employees are open to feedback and constructive criticism.

1   2   3   4   5

Employees are aware of and adhere to policies, regulations and standards.

1   2   3   4   5

The ACT of Change Management

Employees practice good customer service and show courtesy to consumers.

1   2   3   4   5

Employees are quality-oriented when it comes to their work.

1   2   3   4   5

The team values differences of opinion and an open flow of ideas.

1   2   3   4   5

Employees communicate well and vent up, instead of outward.

1   2   3   4   5

Employees work well under pressure and stress.

1   2   3   4   5

There is forgiveness for past hurts among the employees.

1   2   3   4   5

There is strong collaboration amongst team members.

1   2   3   4   5

Employees feel that they can openly and honestly express themselves.

1   2   3   4   5

When completed, add up your total score, then mark your score as an X on the line below.

```
----------------------------------------------------------------
20          40          60          80          100
```

Toxic \Entitlement   Positive/Achievement

Analysis

Where did you mark your X? Your results will give you a snapshot of workplace culture at the present time. It will also reveal how far you need to go on your change journey. For example, if department A scored 85, that would indicate that the change leader needs to focus more on maintenance and keeping positive momentum. However if program B scored 41, that would indicate that the change leader has a long way to go in terms of promoting positive culture change. The change leader for program B would need to consider an intense focus of resources towards performance management and the empowerment of employees.

The Significance Of Workplace Culture

Not only does the change leader need to assess each of their employees, they must also be able to assess the culture in their organizations. Every organization has its own culture; even within an organization, there may be several subcultures found in specific departments, teams or even shifts. The question to consider is: why is it so important to assess culture? The understanding of workplace culture is critically important for the following reasons:

It represents the common beliefs, values and meanings shared by the employees in that particular setting.

It is usually understood but rarely spoken of openly by employees.

It is pervasive and has a powerful influence on the behavior of employees.

It will help the change leader determine how to motivate employees.

The ACT of Change Management

How the change leader responds to the culture will often predict their success or failure in promoting positive change.

Changing the culture is not easy by any means. A common belief among change leaders is that their priority is to "change the culture" of the organization. However, this belief is in error. Kotter (2002) states that in the process of promoting change, culture is actually one of the last things to change, not the first. According to Kotter, the change leader must focus on convincing employees to change their own individual behaviors first. If employees change their behavior then the culture inevitably will begin to shift from negative to positive.

Instead of trying to change the culture, the change leader must first understand the culture they have "inherited." Then they should assess employee's aptitude and achievement—employing the techniques detailed in the last chapter—in order to promote positive behavior change. In other words, workplace culture is something that every change leader must keep in the back of their minds but not necessarily act on directly on a daily basis. Every change leader who assumes a management role inherits certain personnel. No doubt the new change leader will give each employee a blank slate and a chance to prove themselves based on their performance and conduct. However, the question remains: if you had to re-interview each employee you inherited in your organization, according to your standards and principles, how many of them would you have actually hired?

This is a very sobering concept. Most change leaders that I have posed this question to typically respond that they would not have hired upward of 50% of their employees. This naturally leads one to consider the importance of good recruiting. Good recruiting is so vitally important because it is better to get the right people up front so that you can prevent having to performance manage them later on.

Strategic Recruiting

It is highly recommended that upon being hired, every new change leader make it a priority to closely examine the interview questions that the organization has used in the past to recruit new employees. If those interview questions are not reflective of the high performance and principles that you would expect as a change leader, then they must be changed. Much has been written about how to recruit good employees and it is not worthwhile to go into too much depth on this here. However, each change leader must closely assess the following in each prospective candidate:

> Education
> Knowledge base
> Skills
> Experience

Most of these can be clearly gleaned from a resume; however, there are certain "intangibles" that do not appear on a resume and which require more investigation on the part of the change leader during the interview. Often, what the change leader sees on paper is not necessarily what is presented at the actual interview. Obviously, candidates embellish their resume, but the change leader must also find ways to ascertain the following:

> Judgment
> Decision making

It is arguable whether these two criteria are actually more important to assess than the first four. Judgment and decision making can be assessed by posing scenario and critical analysis questions to the interviewee. These types of questions force the candidate to think on their feet and allow the interviewer to observe the candidate's thought process.

Another critically important consideration is whether or not that candidate is going to fit into the culture of the workplace. If the candidate is a new graduate with little experience and the workplace culture in which they will be working is toxic, it is the equivalent of throwing fresh meat to hungry sharks. Those new grads will no doubt be forced to find ways to survive, and they are at risk of being poisoned by the culture. On the other hand, older, more experienced candidates also carry the risk of "baggage," or old habits they may have picked up in other places. They could also do a lot of damage when hired, as they can be a very negative influence on the culture. In order to allow the change leader to better assess if a candidate will be able to cope with the culture in an organization, the scenario and critical analysis questions can reflect real life scenarios that reveal things like communication style, leadership and conflict resolution.

High Risk High Reward

I recall a conversation between two managers. The first had accomplished tremendous success in performance managing their employees and subsequently transforming the culture of their workplace by holding employees accountable for their performance and conduct. This manager and his team went through many struggles and hardships, but in the end the sacrifices paid off. The other manager, who was facing similar problems with a toxic culture she inherited, was asking the first manager for advice. After the meeting I learned that the second manager went off and started changing processes and practices in the belief that it would ultimately change the culture in her department. However, the second manager's plan for change did not involve any risk on her part and nothing that would involve holding employees directly accountable for their behavior; she was anticipating pushback and resistance. However, she failed to realize that in order to challenge culture, you must first challenge behavior.

Eventually, all the policies and practices she put in place failed to make any significant impact because she did not directly address the issue of culture. The culture in her department was hostile and toxic. Whenever she tried to institute the new practices and policies the toxic employees ultimately undermined them.

Here are the contrasts between Entitlement Culture vs. Achievement Culture:

Entitlement Culture	**Achievement Culture**
Management owes employee	Employee owes the client
Rejection of education and skill building	Actively engaged in education and skills upgrading
Status quo oriented	Progressive and forward thinking

Extrinsically oriented (reward-motivated)	Intrinsically oriented (self-motivated)
Paranoia and mistrust	Trusting
Bullying and harassment	Respect for all
Negative cohesion (employees like a family)	Positive cohesion (employees like a team)
Comfort and convenience oriented	Positive risk taking
Unaccountable	Accountable
Closed minded and un-teachable	Open minded and teachable
Disdains and avoids feedback	Seeks feedback and constructive criticism
Ignorance of and non-compliance with standards	Aware of and compliant with standards
Poor customer service	Excellent customer service
Does the bare minimum	Quality oriented; i.e., goes the extra mile
Values conformity	Values individual team member diversity
Vents outwards to peers	Vents up to superiors
Collapses under pressure and stress	Perseveres through adversity
Holds grudges	Forgives past hurts
Every man for himself	Collaborative
Silences those who attempt to be progressive	Permission for self-expression

Family Versus Team

On her first day of work, a new change leader was greeted by a employee who proudly stated that the team was like a family. This sounded good until the change leader began to understand what that actually meant. In this context, family was not a positive attribute but a negative one. To illustrate there are the Walton's and then there are the Manson's. It all depends on how one defines the term "family." The change leader in this example later uncovered serious issues of misconduct that were below the surface and not apparent to most people. Family in this sense was more like a culture of organized crime: squeal and we'll get you. Employees who tried to speak out were crushed and bullied by the employees who held the power and influence. In stark contrast, a "team" is a far better concept. Teams, by definition, achieve goals, whereas families typically do not. Teams are focused on improvement and performance whereas family is oriented more towards comfort and security.

Bridging The Gap

The question that must be asked is: "how does a change leader transform a culture of entitlement into a culture of achievement?" The answer is standards. For example, let's suppose a change leader is faced with a culture in which there are problems with absenteeism. Upon deeper investigation, it is discovered that arriving to work late or making illegitimate sick calls is a common practice among employees because the change leader's predecessor looked the other way when this issue came up and did not address it. Then the employees concluded that this behavior is acceptable and so it persists. This also supports the concept that workplace culture is unspoken, but understood. I am sure in this case that the employees are not openly speaking about calling in sick when they want a day off. They just go ahead and do it because they have been conditioned to believe it is acceptable.

If the new change leader attempts to remedy this by performance managing the employees, they will no doubt cry foul and cite the fact that the predecessor accepted the behavior. What will ultimately help the change leader is a policy concerning absenteeism, with which he or she can enforce and hold the employees accountable.

Shaking Up The Culture

In his book "Unspeakable," author Os Guinness discusses the concept of abuse of power. He claims that there are two primary themes involved: deception and coercion (Guinness. 2005). In some labor management settings, deception means that those employees who hold power and influence actively deny that there is anything wrong that needs to be changed. So when the change leader arrives and talks about things like enhancing skills, professional conduct and improving customer service, these individuals often agree and then claim that they are already living up to and practicing those standards. However, when the change leader begins to implement change, it often involves turning over rocks and shining a light on poor practices and conduct that have been long been hidden. When these issues become exposed, those same employees then turn to coercion. They begin to "step on the throats" of others who agree with the positive changes, in an effort to silence them through threats of intimidation.

Case Example

Diane is a twenty-five-year veteran who appears on the surface to be pleasant, polite and client focused. Diane likes to talk about the "good old days" when the employees were like a family. In employee meetings, she appears to endorse positive practices. However, it comes to the attention of the change leader that Diane has another side that is not as obvious. The more the change leader exposes poor practices and conduct, the more he notices that other employees appear, through their body language, to be very intimidated by Diane. The change leader suspects something is wrong and attempts to engage the threatened employees, but most appear hesitant to report Diane's behavior due to fear of retaliation. It isn't until one brave employee breaks the silence that the change leader learns that Diane has been threatening employees behind the change leaders back, reminding them that they are unionized employees and that they should not be "snitches," or rat on each other.

The change leader then decides to confront Diane and objectively brings her attention to the organizations code of conduct, which prohibits intimidation and encourages people to report poor practice and conduct. Diane nods her head and agrees, stating that she has been there 25 years, and that if she sees poor practice she goes up to the person performing poorly and tells them directly.

On the surface, Diane and the change leader appear to now be on the same page, don't they? But Diane is a master manipulator. Notice how she skillfully says that if she becomes aware of poor practice and conduct that she would tell the person directly. However, what she does not say is that she would report it to her superiors. This illustrates clearly that, when the change leader attempts to upset the status quo, people will often show their true colors. Those who stand to lose the most by being exposed will respond by first deceiving the change leader into thinking they are positive employees. However, as the veil over poor practice and conduct is lifted, those individuals often turn to coercion and bullying their colleagues into maintaining silence, and the status quo.

For many change leaders, this is perhaps the hardest thing to do. To go against the grain and threaten to disrupt people's comfort level risks making the leader very unpopular. It is far easier to remain silent and maintain the status quo. To challenge the status quo means to stick your neck out. Based on this, I offer a new definition of leadership: being willing to stand on your principles and then accepting the consequences of taking that stand.

If doing the right thing meant that it would make you unpopular, would you still do it? How much would you be willing to risk? If the change leader is going to upset the accepted order in an organization, he or she must first be prepared to challenge the status quo in their own leadership style. This inevitably involves taking risks.

Case Example

A new management team was brought into a healthcare facility that had a longstanding poor reputation in the community. The new management team held a 3-day retreat to do strategic planning aimed turning the organization around. They began by identifying the status quo, or what the employees felt was acceptable. The list they generated was shocking, to say the least, and included the following:

- Client abuse

- Poor care approach by nursing employees

- Neglect of personal cares

- Increased complaints

- Clients medically unstable

- Client's weight loss

- Client's increased hospital transfers

- Increased medication errors

- Lack of documentation

- Increased critical incidents

- Lack of thorough assessments

- Poor leadership

- Short staffing

- Increased risk to patients

- Poor interactions with families

- Task focused care

- Employees not willing to do the extra

The management team employed ACT in the following way:

Assertive—they were honest with perceptions of each other, even if it meant they would cause hurt and strain relationships.

Collaborative—they started doing team building exercises to build stronger relationships.

Transparent—they were willing to be vulnerable; i.e., the top executive encouraged employee to write down their perceptions of him and listened while they openly discussed the problems they had with him. This took tremendous courage on the part of the senior executive, but it helped him to better understand how he was being viewed by his own leadership team. It also allowed him to correct many of the misconceptions his own managers had of him. Those misperceptions were put on the table and this discourse became the tipping point, on the day two of the retreat. This senior executive truly lived the aforementioned leadership definition. He made the tough call by allowing himself to be vulnerable and transparent; then he stood there to take the hit, in the form of criticism from his own team. How many change leaders today would be willing to do that?

Kotter talks about creating a sense of urgency. The management team in this example had to first define what needed to change first (the status quo) and agree that it needed to be changed before they could move forward.

Persuasion To Change

Appealing to the emotions of employees has proven to be a significant factor in shifting the culture in an organization by positively persuading employees to change their own behavior.

This leads to this very important concept from John Kotter (2002):

"People change what they do less because they are given analysis that shifts their thinking than because they are shown a truth that influences their feelings."

To better understand how this plays out, I will illustrate the point by borrowing a philosophical construct that involves three levels (Zacharias. 2007).

Persuasion & Argument

      Level one: Logical (cognitive, or the intellectual argument)

      Level two: Expressive (how that argument is expressed)

      Level three: Prescriptive (how one applies that argument)

There are three levels of persuasion. To illustrate: let's say that I want to give my teenager the advice to stay away from drugs.

I could simply just tell her that drugs are bad for her and argue at level one, which would be ineffective. Or, I could tell her to stay away from kids who do drugs and who could end up being a bad influence. That would be me prescribing a course of action. Would that be effective? No. However, let's suppose my teenager has a school friend who uses drugs and experiences problems at home and I sit down with my teenager and ask them to talk about their feelings. Would that have more of a significant influence on her behavior? Yes. This illustrates that the most profound behavioral change occurs at the emotional level.

Let me illustrate again, using a real life example:

Several years ago, a well known newspaper ran a series on client abuse in long-term care homes. What they found was a shocking number neglect cases in numerous homes. The exposure from the newspaper series, combined with a television news program, heightened awareness and touched people and politicians at an emotional level, provoking action. To use the 3 factor philosophical framework, the issue could be framed this way:

> Level one: Logical—client abuse is bad
>
> Level two: Expressive - news media coverage
>
> Level three: Prescriptive - increased public campaigns and awareness, resulting in a change in legislation

In other words, when the public was shown shocking photos of neglect and video evidence of physical abuse, it moved them to action. In turn, the government was compelled to respond by introducing new legislation and government inspections of long-term care homes.

"Tipping" Towards Change

Contagion

Malcolm Gladwell's 2002 book *The Tipping Point* makes the point that social trends and changes often come about by word of mouth or contagion. In fact, many social psychologists have conducted research on the phenomena of contagion theory. To illustrate, on one occasion I was flying home after delivering a presentation at a conference in the fall of 2009. This was during the peak of the H1N1 pandemic, which was spreading across the globe and into North America. There was a case in which a young boy reportedly collapsed and died at a hockey game in Ontario. That story traveled right across Canada through word of mouth. As I sat in the airport lounge, almost everyone was reading the newspaper and talking about it. That concern soon turned into anxiety and immunizations clinics became clogged with long lineups of worried parents and their children. The anxiety over H1N1 proved to be highly contagious and had a profound effect on people's behaviors.

Sudden Shift

In a crisis, there is always some catalytic event that threatens to become culture changing. That event causes people to question old ways of doing things and creates the need to improve, sometimes because public safety is at stake. The attacks of September 11, 2001 permanently changed air travel. Never before were people who relied on regular air travel required to pass through so many security check points. Tighter measures were put in place to detect potential threats from people and objects such as luggage, laptops and electronic devices. The threat of hijacking and terrorism forced airports and customs agents to change the way they operated. Similarly, Sudden Acute Respiratory Syndrome (SARS), which became a critical epidemic in 2002, and it permanently changed infection control in the healthcare system. Like the security measures in airports from 9/11, hospitals and clinics were forced to step up with massive changes to hygiene practices and procedures. These were events that support Gladwell's concept that change usually happens dramatically, in one moment, instead of gradually.

Making Small Changes

Gladwell also makes the important point that sometimes little actions can result in big effects. This coincides with Pareto's concept of focusing on the 20%, or an even smaller proportion. Like dropping a pebble into a pond, which results in large ripples, sometimes small changes made by the change leader can have a profound long-term effect on the organization, thus initiating positive change. This is also a radically different from the traditional thinking, which tends to focus on making big changes. In fact, the opposite is true. Gladwell uses the concept of "broken window theory." He uses the example of crime in the New York subways in late 1970's and early 1980's. By changing the physical environment of the subways, public officials changed public perception and crime was drastically reduced. Broken window theory states that if a person continually sees a broken window that never gets fixed, he or she will begin to believe that no one cares and that there are no consequences for such acts. In the New York City example, by making small changes, they changed public perception and restored public trust by cracking down on turnstile jumpers and graffiti. They gave the perception that someone was in control and that put commuters at ease.

Now apply this to the workplace. Suppose that a change leader is experiencing a toxic culture in which there appears to be a form of anarchy or defiance of rules among the employees. Using the broken window concept, it is safe to assume that the majority of employees in such a circumstance do not agree with the negative ringleaders who are responsible for the situation. The longer the anarchy persists, the more the silent majority will lose faith in order and come to accept that lawlessness is the norm. If the change leader were to make small changes, such as enforcing dress code and punctuality, that might create the perception that someone is in charge and that things are coming under control.

The 2000 film *Remember the Titans* illustrates these concepts nicely. The film takes place in 1970's Virginia, several years into the aftermath of the civil rights unrest in the southern United States. T.C. Williams is a high school that has chosen to integrate black and white students, and the result is tension and conflict. This ultimately filters down to the football team, which also becomes integrated. Denzel Washington plays Herman Boone, the black head coach charged with managing the unrest among the players while trying to lead the team to a state championship. The most poignant part of the film involves Boone taking the players on a long run in the middle of the night to the civil war site of Gettysburg. There, he delivers a moving speech, claiming that the team can come together, or it can risk being destroyed. That moment is the point at which things shift and the team decides to unite. The result lines up with the true story of the T.C. Williams Titans, who went undefeated that season and went on to win the state championship. The key to that result is that Boone appealed not to the intellect of the team, but to their emotions, and this motivated them to change.

Review Of Key Principles

Workplace culture

- It represents the common beliefs, values and meaning shared by the employees in that particular setting.

- It is usually understood but rarely spoken about openly by the employees.

- It is pervasive and has a powerful influence on the behavior of the employees.

- It will help the change leader know how to motivate the employees.

- How the change leader responds to the culture will often predict their success or failure in promoting positive change.

Strategic recruiting is important to preventing problem employees down the road.

Changing the culture involves risks for the change leader who attempts to shake up the culture and upset the accepted order.

Adherence to standards allows the change leader to bridge the gap between an entitlement culture to an achievement culture.

A new definition of leadership: being willing to stand on your principles, and then accepting the consequences for taking that stand.

Persuading workers to change involves the change leader reaching the employees at an emotional level.

The more contagious the vision and message, the more likely it will spread and stick with employees.

Change sometimes happens dramatically instead of gradually.

Small changes often make a significant difference down the road.

CHAPTER 6

The ACT of Empowerment

A great deal has been written about empowering employees. The vast wealth of information makes this a difficult subject to tackle because so much has been written in leadership books, presented by motivational speakers and made available through the internet. The question is: what new information does the ACT model offer concerning empowerment?

The ACT Of "Dis-empowerment?"

To address this issue, I am going to take a unique approach and present the opposite, which is "how to dis-empower people." After having worked for an autocratic boss, I reflected on that experience and found that it taught me "how *not* to manage people." When I speak in front of audiences, I commonly ask for a show of hands of those who have had to survive under a tyrannical or heavy-handed employer. In every instance, I estimate at least 80% of the hands in the room go up. What is more interesting is the way the audience's facial expression and body language suddenly changes when they recall that experience. Some people nod their heads as if to silently say "yep, I know what that was like." Others cross their arms in a defensive posture and remain silent. Regardless, it always evokes an emotional reaction; the experience is so vivid that most can recall it like it was yesterday, even though it may have happened a decade ago. Neuroscience tells us that the memories we can recall the most vividly are often the ones that often a powerful memory attached to it. In the case of the disempowered, that experience can be so traumatic that sometimes it can hardly be forgotten, even after the passing of many years.

So why is it that so many have encountered this experience? Why don't 80% of the hands in a room go up to indicate the opposite experience of working for an empowering boss? Why is the autocratic boss so pervasive in the workforce? There is no clear cut answer to this question. Perhaps the answer lies not in the individual boss but in the culture that cultivates a negative boss.

<u>Military Influences</u>

There are many themes associated with traditional leadership that are tied to the military, such as:

> Emphasis on punctuality
>
> Expectations of neatness and uniformity
>
> Use of terms like subordinate or insubordination
>
> Discipline as a reaction to bad behavior
>
> Chain of command structure
>
> Emphasis on developing toughness through adversity
>
> Low tolerance for underachievement
>
> Development of "strategic plans"

What follows is merely an observation and is not intended to demean the military in any way or to criticize the sacrifices made by men and women in the armed forces. In fact, one could argue that such principles are still necessary in today's workplace. Can you imagine a workplace in which there was no standard for attire, penalty for lateness or expectation for good behaviors? Yet, the opposite, a strict culture, gave rise to the "drill sergeant." That person's sole purpose is to break down the new recruit and mold them into a fighting soldier by building mental and physical toughness. In this situation, the means—hazing, verbal abuse, brutal discipline and humiliation—are seen as justified by the end, and so are considered acceptable forms of training. In fact, to survive basic training is an expectation and considered an achievement in military culture. Imagine a newly recruited private filing an harassment and bullying charge against his or her drill sergeant. Such a thought is laughable.

The emphasis in such a culture is on results and not so much the process or means by which the results are attained. To continue with this example, the superior of the drill sergeant is not likely to be concerned with "how" the drill sergeant trains the recruits, but rather that he accomplishes his objective and produces soldiers ready to fight. One could argue that we would not want a solider that has not been able to survive the adversity of boot camp and basic training. For instance, what might a new soldier do when faced with the hardships of combat if basic training instead happened at a tropical resort with a personal trainer?

If we apply this now to the modern workforce, we see that we have adopted a similar "ends justifies the means" mentality. I recall encountering a senior official with one particular organization. The employees who worked under this individual were visibly frustrated and would openly complain to one another when the boss was not around. As a consultant, I remember trying to professionally disagree with this boss; I presented paper evidence to support my argument, only to have her dismiss it outright. I once sat in on an employee's meeting that she chaired and that included all of her management team. She was attempting to problem solve an issue that had recently been raised. For the entire hour long meeting, she was the only one who spoke. The rest of the team sat silent and almost terrified, with no one daring to say a word in disagreement with her. She concluded the meeting by re-stating the plan of action that she felt they all agreed upon. The only problem was that no one actually agreed to the plan, because no one had spoken.

I then witnessed employee after employee resign from the organization. Surely the corporate head office would take note that this tyrannical boss was causing problems with employee retention? However, I learned differently when I ran into a peer of that tyrannical boss from another organization that was under the same corporation. In passing conversation, the tyrannical boss's name was raised and the peer began to rave about her, citing her reputation for getting results and achieving operational efficiency. There was my answer. In my opinion (and without actually interviewing anyone from the corporate office), it did not appear to matter how this boss treated her employees. What mattered was that she got results; and by the way, she was very much a drill sergeant.

Traditional Hierarchical Structure

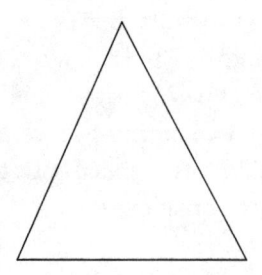

The more control an employee is given, the higher their quality of work life. The triangle typically represents the hierarchical organization wherein the person at the top sends orders down to the next level and so on and so on, until it finally reaches the frontline worker. How much influence does the frontline worker have on his or her job in this structure? How much can the frontline worker impact organizational changes at a higher level? In fact, studies in communication have proven that top-down communication causes numerous problems, including information at the top being withheld from people at the bottom, sometimes for insidious reasons. Alternatively, filtering becomes another problem; i.e., information travelling down the hierarchy gets distorted or changed by the time it gets to the frontline worker. It is easy, now, to see that the traditional hierarchical structure is a fertile breeding ground for both the autocratic boss and the disempowered employee.

More organizations are attempting to flip the triangle upside down so that the frontline employee is now at the top and has more control over his or her destiny, while the senior officials are at the bottom of the triangle. This is not to say that senior officials are not important, but it represents a relinquishment of power and a shared governance model that values the frontline employee.

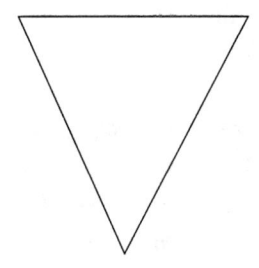

Selfless Leadership

In their book *The 5 Patterns of Extraordinary Careers: The Guide for Achieving Success and Satisfaction*, authors James Citrin and Richard Smith propose that the most successful leaders in the corporate world are those who have been able to benefit from the talents of the people around them, such as their peers, subordinates and superiors. In other words, it is the people around them who make them great, not the other way around. According to their research, the most successful executives exhibits a selflessness and concern for the success of others over that of themselves. Their conclusion is that these "benevolent leaders" create an environment of high retention, in which employees want to work and perform their best for the leader. In return they reward the leader with loyalty and productivity.

This concept of selfless leadership seems counter to the cultural in today's workplace. So much emphasis is put on rugged individualism, as well as an ambitious and competitive style of leadership that traditionally rewards those who can successfully claw their way to the top. If this means stepping on others to get to the top, then that leader will do that to achieve their goals; but this is done at the risk of disempowering those underneath him. In the long run that leader will have a difficult time retaining employees. Such leaders also tend to cling to power, as opposed to sharing it. Again, this is common in the traditional triangle hierarchy. This type of leader may see aspiring leaders as competition and may actually discourage or hold them down instead of empowering them. This is occurs most often because empowering those employees may mean that one day they might exceed the leader and displace him or her. This type of leader may allow aspiring leaders to achieve, but might also then take credit for their work.

The question every leader must be willing to ask themselves is whether or not they are willing to work themselves out of a job.

What if the aspiring employee underneath you was to outperform you? Are you willing to take the risk that helping others achieve may actually cost you in the long run? These are not easy questions to answer, but a leader who seeks to be selfless must struggle with them if he or she is to truly empower others. And the selfless leader who puts others first will inevitably be the true winner in the long run. The reason for this is that they will be more likely to inspire loyalty from their employees, and by developing aspiring leaders, they will benefit from the new ideas that those new leaders will develop. In other words, their subordinates will make *the leader* a better leader.

Your Blind Spot

To refer back again to an example used above, I may ask the audience if any of them have ever experienced road rage when, for example, they were accidentally cut off while driving. You can visualize this by imagining two cars driving in the same direction in lanes beside one another. If one of those cars is slightly behind the other car's mirrors then that car is in the other car's blind spot i.e., Car A cannot see car B, but car B can see car A.

If car A suddenly realizes that their right hand turn is coming up and they are about to miss it, they might abruptly make a right turn and inadvertently cut off car B. Car B then responds by leaning on the horn, making a rude hand gesture or cursing. Did car A deliberately cut off car B? The answer is no. In order to believe that, you would also have to believe that car A had spent the last week analyzing car B, as well as traffic patterns, in an attempt to determine the exact moment to cut off car B, just so they could ruin car B's day. Naturally, that assumption would be absurd. In essence, car A was not deliberately doing anything against car B. In fact, car A was focused on meeting its own need.

In leadership management it is crucial that every leader learn their blind spot. The Johari Window is a great tool that defines a blind spot in terms of the information others knows about the leader and of which the leader is unaware. I remember an intense meeting with two colleagues. The purpose of the meeting was to discuss documents that had gone missing and it appeared as though one of my two colleagues may have accidentally lost them. After the meeting, one colleague told the other that she did not like the way I was looking at them in the meeting. She felt that my facial expression and eyes were accusing her. When I reflect on that incident, I can honestly say that I did not intend to come across that way. I felt I was just concentrating on what my colleague was saying. However, my intense look may have given another impression.

This illustrates the blind spot concept perfectly. There was information about myself of which I was unaware and that others perceived. It became a great lesson for me to check my facial expression in meetings. For the change leader, it is important that they discover and check their blind spot. Like the driver who forgets to check his mirrors and look over his shoulder, many leaders go through life "cutting people off" and being completely unaware that they are doing so. So this begs the question: how do I discover my blind spot?

The simplest and most effective way to do this is to actually ask someone who you trust to give you honest and constructive feedback. This is not an easy thing to do, as it requires one to be willing to be made vulnerable. Here are some questions that might help:

Do other people see me in a way that I am not aware?

Do I have behaviors or body language that could be misinterpreted in a negative way?

In terms of interpersonal interactions, are there areas where I might be offending others that I need to be aware of?

One lady came up to me after a seminar and told me that her colleagues at work did not get along with her. Her comment was, "they don't like me." I asked her why they might feel that way. She responded, "they think that I am angry at them." As she was saying this, her face tightened, her eyes sharpened and her brow furrowed into a menacing look, while her body language gestured in hostility. I very diplomatically told her that if I was to hold up a mirror and allow her to see herself, she would understand why her colleagues may perceive her that way.

Steve Mathew

The change leader must be aware of how they are perceived. Even if a change leader communicates positive messages, if their mannerisms, body language and behavior show the exact opposite, then it confuses people and detracts from the leader's credibility. Ultimately, to promote any positive change, the change leader must be seen as trustworthy and sensitive to the people around them; that is, if they are to successfully gain buy in for their vision. The blind spot will be discussed more in later chapters.

<u>Don't Cross The Boss</u>

Many of us, as leaders, go through our day "cutting people off" at work and ignoring our blind spot. We might be offending the people who work under us and not even know it. How many of our subordinates would actually dare confront the boss about a comment made or an action that offended them? Most would probably say nothing and then complain to themselves or others. Why would they not say anything? If we return to the military themes and triangle hierarchy, we can see that the unspoken rule in the workplace is "don't cross the boss."

However, any selfless leader would probably want the feedback denied by that attitude, but may not know how to ask for it. So, how does a leader discover their blind spot?

Johari Window

In 1955 Joseph Luft and Harry Ingham created a heuristic that mapped out the following:

	4. known to self	3. unknown to self
1. known to others	Public Self	Blind Spot
2. unknown to others	Private Self	Subconscious Mind

The ACT of Change Management

According to Luft and Ingham there are four quadrants:

> 1. *Information known to self and others:* **Public Self**

> This is the part of ourselves that we choose to reveal to others. Often, this might include certain personality traits, preferences, hobbies or interests. We deem this information to be "innocent" and sharing it with others is low-risk.

> 2. *Information that is known to self but not known to others:* **Private Self**

> No one shares everything about themselves with others. There are always some things about ourselves that we deem inappropriate or private and that we do not wish to share with others. This information may be deemed as more high risk when shared, as it may change the way people perceive us or our reputation.

> 3. *Information that is unknown to self and unknown to others:* **Subconscious Mind**

> This could be revealed if you were put into a situation that is unanticipated or unforeseen, so that you might not know how you would react.

> 4. *Information that is unknown to self and known to others:* **Blind Spot**

> This is what others see in you and what you are not able to see yourself. In leadership management this is a key concept that must be grasped. Every leader has, in their mind, a picture of the way they think they are perceived; but in reality, this may differ greatly from the way in which a leader is actually perceived.

For example, I once encountered a new leader who was struggling with conflicts among certain members of the team. This new leader was a very pleasant person with a calm demeanor. However, there were individuals on the team who did not respond to the new leader's approach. It turned out that when there was a disagreement, the new leader felt threatened and stood his ground against those who challenged him. On many occasions he was justified in doing so, but he was unaware that others on the team were observing that he was actually raising his voice and being argumentative. When I confronted him about this, he truly did not think he was engaging in power struggles or being adversarial. Yet the employees who observed him said the opposite. I was able to use the Johari Window as a framework to help coach this new leader by allowing him to see that the feedback could be used constructively and was illustrating his blind spot. We then began a process of goal setting aimed at helping him become aware of his blind spot and learning ways to cope and compensate for it. Through role playing, we were able to identify situations of conflict, and through that process the new leader realized that he perceived employee disagreement with his decisions as a vote of non-confidence in his leadership. He would then get his "back up" and defend his position, not aware that he was being drawn into a power struggle. By becoming aware of his blind spot, he able to recognize power struggle situations and to then adjust his approach to be more collaborative and less adversarial.

Multiple Source Feedback

How can a leader determine his or her blind spot if they cannot objectively assess their own behavior? One way is to gather the information informally, which would involve asking a trusted colleague to give you open and honest feedback. Then engage in some self-reflection and plan strategies for self-improvement. Another way to do this is through a formal assessment; but the most recommended means to determine your blind spot is a process known as 360 degree feedback. If we return to the concept of the "selfless leader," you will recall that the most successful leaders are those who have been able to benefit from the talents of the people around them, such as their peers, subordinates and superiors. In a 360 degree assessment, the individuals who would rate you as a leader would be:

    Your superiors (the people above you)

    Your peers (the people who work beside you)

    Your direct reports (the people who work under you)

Those are the individuals required to give an anonymous and well-rounded (360 degree) assessment of your performance. This comes from a variety of different perspectives that combine to produce a complete picture of how one is perceived by others. Usually, 3 people from each category are recommended, but the more that participate, the richer the assessment results.

Such a process can prove to be very uncomfortable for many in leadership positions, especially if they receive feedback from their direct reports. This process requires the leader to be completely vulnerable and open to criticism. This is a very eye opening experience, as the results may challenge the way in which a leader perceives him or herself by providing a picture of how others actually see them. Because we acknowledged that many frontline employees refrain from giving their boss direct feedback about their behavior, an anonymous computerized process allows them to comment freely and honestly, without any fear of reprisal.

The next logical question is: who should be chosen to respond among the leader's direct reports? If we return to assessing achievement and aptitude (discussed in chapter four), recall that there were three groups of employees:

> Positive (Change Agents)
>
> Neutral (Status Quo)
>
> Negative (Instigators/Burnouts)

What are the pros and cons of each group? Choosing only positive employees that like you will likely provide a biased assessment that would yield unbalanced and inaccurately favorable results. Conversely, choosing negative employees would yield unbalanced and inaccurately unfavorable results. Logically, then, the people who would provide the most balanced assessment would be the Status Quo group. Often, these individuals are very perceptive and observant. They often have insights about a leader that they would not regularly share but that would be helpful in identifying and overcoming their leader's blind spot.

The Coaching Relationship

In the healthcare field, the concept of the healthcare provider-patient relationship is very important. This is sometimes referred to as the "therapeutic relationship." Therapeutic, in this sense, means "helping" and not necessarily doing psychotherapy. I am going to borrow this analogy in order to illustrate some similarities and themes that can be compared to the relationship between coach and employee.

In healthcare, practitioners are taught that a therapeutic relationship between them and the patient is based on several components:

- Trust
- Empathy
- Shared Goals
- Power
- Non-Judgmental Attitude
- Maintenance of Professional Distance

Practitioners who model these qualities are often able to get even the most challenging and resistant patients to do things that others could not. Similarly, coaching is all about motivation, and an effective coach can motivate an employee by displaying and practicing similar qualities. These themes are captured in the "Coaching Relationship Self-Assessment" include in this chapter. It is important that every coach engage in some reflection and assess themselves, in addition to becoming familiar with some of the important themes associated with the coaching relationship.

COACHING Relationship - SELF Assessment

Instructions:

Identify an employee who you are currently coaching, or a future leader who you feel will be ready for a specific role, project or task. Using the following criteria, please rate your level of confidence in your skills when it comes to interacting with this individual.

1) Professionalism
Maintaining a professional demeanor and a rational detachment when working with your employee on sensitive issues:

Not at all				Very confident
1	2	3	4	5

2) Enablement
Empowering your employee to be independent and to operate as autonomously as possible:

Not at all				Very confident
1	2	3	4	5

3) Flexibility
Adjusting task or project parameters to set up your employee for success.

Not at all				Very confident
1	2	3	4	5

4) Resolving tensions
Repairing problems with the employee as an ongoing process.

Not at all				Very confident
1	2	3	4	5

5) Environment
Creating a positive and supportive work culture that enables the growth of your employee.

    Not at all   Very confident

      1   **2**   **3**   **4**   **5**

6) Employee self-expression
Allowing the employee to openly express their feelings and ideas:

    Not at all   Very confident

      1   **2**   **3**   **4**   **5**

7) Listening
Listening non-judgmentally and with openness when your employee makes mistakes.

    Not at all   Very confident

      1   **2**   **3**   **4**   **5**

8) Emotional states
Recognizing emotional states and changes in mood, including behavior cues that indicate stress in the employee.

    Not at all   Very confident

      1   **2**   **3**   **4**   **5**

9) Confrontation
Assertively confronting negative behaviors or poor productivity.

    Not at all   Very confident

      1   **2**   **3**   **4**   **5**

10) Empathy

Empathizing with the employee's feeling states and conveying understanding when they are struggling.

Not at all   Very confident

1   2   3   4   5

11) Consistency

Maintaining a consistent approach with all employees and avoiding the appearance of favoritism towards the employee.

Not at all   Very confident

1   2   3   4   5

12) Creativity

Enabling the employee to bring their own creativity and innovation to the role, project or task.

Not at all   Very confident

1   2   3   4   5

13) Roadblocks

Identifying and addressing potential threats (people, situations, level of experience) that might cause the employee to fail in their role, project or task.

Not at all   Very confident

1   2   3   4   5

14) Debriefing

Turning negative experience into a teachable moment for your employee.

Not at all   Very confident

1   2   3   4   5

15) Fostering understanding
Actively listening and enabling the employee to understand you and your expectations.

Not at all   **Very confident**

1   **2**   **3**   **4**   **5**

Reflection

1) In what areas did you rate yourself as most confident?
2) In what areas did you rate yourself as least confident?
3) What do you need to do to achieve a more therapeutic relationship with your clients?

Parallel Process Of Coaching

As we saw in the concept of selfless leadership, not only does the coach make the employee better, a good employee also makes the coach better.

Thus, there is a parallel process that occurs: a truly transparent coach, who is interested in attaining feedback concerning their own performance, would not be afraid to ask their employee to use the same criteria to rate themselves. To do so, they can simply use the same survey and substitute the phrase "the employee" with a personal pronoun.

> Example:
>
> 10) Empathizing with **_the employee's_** feeling states and conveying understanding when **_they are_** struggling.
>
> Becomes
>
> 10) Empathizing with **_my_** feeling states and conveying understanding when **_I am_** struggling.

Sam & Carrie: A Case Study of Effective Coaching

Sam was a new manager who began his tenure in a hostile environment wrought with labor-management conflicts. In this particular division, the workplace bully was a female employee known as Margie. Margie had a reputation as an angry burned-out employee who intimidated her colleagues. She was insubordinate to previous managers, bullied and harassed her colleagues and was just as abusive to the customers. In the first year, Sam and Margie clashed numerous times as Margie began to challenge Sam's authority. Margie also began to sabotage many of Sam's projects. The other employees were too afraid to warn Sam or to stand up to Margie, but most felt it was better to align with her rather than challenge her; challenging Margie meant being blackballed and ostracized from the rest of the team.

Carrie was Margie's closest friend and was often caught up in Margie's negativity. Sometimes Carrie also challenged Sam about policies and issues. However, Sam noticed that there was something different about Carrie. When Margie was not working, Carrie was actually seen by the other co-workers as a leader. She typically gave direction to others, worked with great efficiency and provided excellent customer service. However, when she was around Margie she reverted to becoming a follower and joined in the complaining and bitterness.

Sam decided that he would take the time to get to know Carrie better. So he began to initiate impromptu conversations with Carrie. Sam observed that Carrie had a very good sense of humor, so he used that as a common ground and began to joke with her. Sam soon began to schedule meetings to pick Carrie's brain about ideas he had. During the first few meetings Carrie was predictably adversarial but Sam did not take her criticisms personally. He noticed that she actually had some very good insights and rationales for her objections. Sam skillfully began to channel Carrie's complaining into problem solving. During their meetings he would listen to the complaints, but then he would push Carrie for solutions. Before too long their working relationship became much stronger and more collegial and Sam noticed that Carrie's productivity and leadership began to develop even more.

A year passed and the organization announced funding for a new junior leadership program. Sam capitalized on the opportunity and decided that it was time to groom Carrie for a future leadership position. When he first presented the idea Carrie was hesitant. But Sam was persistent and asked Carrie to work with him and allow him to mentor her. He sent Carrie to workshops on leadership and teambuilding skills. This allowed the other co-workers to see that Carrie was working hard to earn the new position, which increased her credibility. Soon after, she interviewed for the new position and was the successful candidate. But what became of Carrie's relationship with Margie? They still remained friends; however, Carrie began to pull away from Margie and actually started to take offense with Margie's behavior because it was bringing down the team. Carrie decided to ignore Margie's complaints and to focus on mentoring the other employees and sharpening her own skills.

In the new role, Carrie was responsible for implementing several new projects and took upon herself the orientation of new employees and students. She excelled in the junior leadership position. Her positive attitude and optimism was instrumental in changing the culture of the division, so much so that the other employees also began to ignore Margie and to walk away from her when she acted out or became negative.

After a year and a half, Sam noticed a posting for a promotion in the organization. He approached Carrie and persuaded her to consider applying for it. Although Sam was sad at the thought of losing Carrie, he realized that she had outgrown and mastered the junior leadership position and was ready to move on to bigger and better responsibilities. Interestingly enough, the position Carrie was interested in was one that Sam had filled himself many years ago. So he mentored her and prepared her for the interview. Carrie, again, excelled in the interview and was offered the job. Sam provided a glowing reference. Although he had lost a tremendous talent, Sam was grateful to Carrie for being the catalyst of the positive turn around within his division.

Ten Principles Of Effective Coaching

Careful analysis of this case reveals many excellent coaching principles:

1. Spotting Potential

Sam was able to see something different in Carrie. An effective coach is one who is able to spot special abilities in certain people. Even the roughest employees may have undeveloped areas in which they might excel. A good coach will identify and develop those abilities further.

2. **Investing Time**

Sam made it a point to have scheduled and unscheduled check-ins with Carrie. He realized that the more time he made for her, the more it would benefit the division in the long run. Effective coaches readily sacrifice their own time to invest in their people.

3. **Providing Ongoing Feedback**

I am sure that in the regular coaching sessions with Carrie, Sam provided ongoing feedback to her about her performance. This is also a mark of a good coach. Effective coaches are always engaging their people and are constantly encouraging them to do better and to improve their performance.

4. **Role Modeling**

Although it is not detailed in this case, Sam's ability to remain objective and handle crisis was very helpful to Carrie. Often, Carrie became the sounding board for the employees to vent their concerns and frustrations about certain decisions made by the organization. During one particular occasion there was a crisis and Carrie, uncertain of what to do, found herself aligning with the employees once again. After the crisis, Sam took the time to debrief with Carrie and constructively admonished her for losing focus and not showing solidarity with him during the crisis. This became a teachable moment that Carrie would not soon forget. Throughout their relationship, Sam had to accept that being unwilling to be unpopular with the employees was an Achilles' heel for Carrie. She realized that as much as she wanted to show that she was supporting her colleagues, it was more important to show leadership and support Sam during crisis.

5. **Being Real**

While role modeling is important, coaches are human and make mistakes too. A temptation for a coach might be to always appear strong and in control. Although the appearance of resolve is very important in building confidence in your leadership, it is also acceptable for coaches to demonstrate vulnerability. Do not be afraid to show emotion, passion or even remorse. If you mess up, fess up. Being too perfect makes you appear aloof and look as though you are setting the bar too high for the person you are coaching. This may have the opposite effect you intend and actually cause frustration.

6. <u>Allowing For Setbacks And Adjusting The plan</u>

In the crisis example above, Sam realized that Carrie did not perform well under the circumstances. Good coaches allow for the fact that the employee might fail in a new role and come up with alternative strategies for success if that is the case.

7. <u>Giving Public Recognition</u>

Sam made it a point to praise Carrie in front of the other workers. Effective coaches will find ways, via emails, employees meetings and other creative ways, to publically praise and recognize their people. This in turn builds their confidence and credibility with the team.

8. <u>Avoiding Being Too Prescriptive</u>

Coaching does not mean always giving a person all the answers to the problems they bring to you. Coaching involves knowing the right questions to ask to help a person come to the solution on their own. If a person arrives at the solution on their own, they are more likely to own it and benefit from the process of problem solving. However, depending on the situation, if a coach knows the answer to a particular problem and the employee is clearly struggling to find the solution, then the coach should not refrain from revealing what might be helpful in that situation.

9. <u>Opening Doors Of Opportunity</u>

The downside of effective coaching is that one can coach someone so well that they risk losing them. In reality, that is a good problem to have. Releasing an employee to pursue a better opportunity means that you, as the coach, helped get them there. It is likely that someone will have done the same for you earlier in your career.

10. Letting Them To Make You Better

As we saw earlier with "selfless leadership," effective coaches learn from the people they coach. Carrie made Sam better at what he did. Carrie brought new ideas to the table and that gave Sam the ability to hone his skills at coaching and mentoring, not to mention the fact that Sam also was the beneficiary of Carrie's exceptional operational performance. She made him look good.

Conclusion

Sam's is an excellent example of using ACT to empower an aspiring leader. He was direct in dealing with Carrie, he was very collaborative—as evidenced by his coaching skills—and then he demonstrated transparency, which solidified the bond of trust between them.

Review of Key Principles

Working under a negative leader can be advantageous because it can teach us how "not to empower people."

A non-traditional hierarchy is the organizational model that best supports empowerment.

A leader who truly believes in empowerment is willing to work him or herself out of a job.

Selfless leaders focus on building others up rather than pursuing their own ambitions.

Selfless leaders allow the people above, beside and below them to make them better.

Effective leaders are aware of their blind spot and develop ways to compensate for it.

Multiple source feedback is an effective way to determine one's blind spot.

The coaching relationship between a change leader and an employee shares similar values to the therapeutic relationship between practitioner and patient in healthcare.

The coaching relationship is a parallel process.

10 Principles of effective coaching include:

1. Spotting potential
2. Investing time
3. Providing ongoing feedback
4. Role modeling
5. Being real
6. Allowing for setbacks and adjusting the plan
7. Giving public recognition
8. Avoiding being too prescriptive
9. Opening doors of opportunity
10. Letting them make you better

CHAPTER 7

THE ACT OF RECOGNITION

In chapter 7 we looked at the importance of assessing employee aptitude and achievement. We discovered that employees generally fall into one of four categories:

    High Aptitude / High Achievement = Change Agents

    Low or Untapped Aptitude / High Achievement = Status Quo

    High Aptitude / Low Achievement = Instigators

    Low Aptitude / Low Achievement = Burnouts

In chapter 6 we looked at ways to empower the "Change Agents." But what do we do with the large majority of employees who fall in the "Status Quo" category? In most organizations the number of people in this category is 60% or higher. They constitute the largest group in any workforce and they are steady producers who might have potential that the change leader has yet to discover or develop. This group must ultimately be persuaded to "up their game." In previous chapters, it was determined that in order to positively affect this group we need to empower the Change Agents, who in turn will push the Status Quos to improve their performance. The two groups combined will then shift the balance of the organization from negative to positive. In sum, that is how organizations change for the better. Ultimately, every change leader should make it their goal to persuade Status Quo employees to become Change Agents by finding their undiscovered potential and by developing their talents and abilities.

Simon & Dean: A Question Of Promotion

Simon and Dean worked together at the same organization for many years. They were close colleagues at work and the best of friends outside of work. They grew up together in the same neighborhood. Simon was a model student; he was a quiet and analytical planner who was always achieving. Dean was the exact opposite: an underachieving student who slacked, but was nonetheless very popular with his peers due to his outgoing personality and sense of humor.

Now in the workplace, the same was true. Simon was the hard working employee who was consistent in his work, never late and rarely absent. His reports were always completed on time and often even submitted before the deadline. He was well respected by his colleagues for his leadership skills and often volunteered to take on new projects. Dean, on the other hand, never handed in his reports on time. He spent much of his time joking around at work and procrastinating. He was popular with clients due to his larger than life personality, but some of his colleagues were unhappy with his laziness. They complained that when they worked with Dean, they had to do their share of the work in addition to his.

To make matters worse, Dean was known as having an anti-management attitude. He often complained about the head office and openly mocked their policies and procedures, even to the point of outright defiance. He had been given written discipline letters for insubordination. Despite this, Dean was very popular with the majority of the employees, due again to his humor and grand personality. He was looked on by many as a rebel hero who had the courage to take on the management.

The time came for the head office to consider employees for promotion, and the question was: which employee got the promotion? The answer was not Simon; it was Dean.

That may shock you as you read this, but some reading this might have guessed that there would be an unexpected twist to the story. The question is: "why?" How could Simon be passed over, given how his track record compared to Dean's?

The answer actually had more to do with the head office than it did with Dean. Dean was an instigator, and the common belief was that the head office saw that Dean had potential and leadership ability (albeit negative). So it was believed that they promoted him in order to make him an ally and to discourage his negative influence on others. The problem was the impact it had on others in the organization, least of whom was Simon. Needless to say, this move created tremendous resentment because most believed Dean did not earn the promotion; it also damaged his credibility. Dean was now viewed as a hypocrite who was anti-management until it was convenient for his own career to sell out his beliefs and became a "company man." Simon left the organization within a year.

This scenario was presented to a management expert for his opinion and he stated that what the organization did was a form of "cheap management." If the head office felt that Dean had potential as a leader, then he should have been made to participate in a leadership program prior to getting the promotion. Optically, it would have allowed others to see that he had earned the position and would have saved some of his credibility, as well as the credibility of the organization. Also, they should have found a way to recognize Simon. In this case the organization did itself a disservice and sent a message to its employees that they were not interested in promoting high performance employees and rewarding hard work. Such a perception serves to de-motivate employees and actually causes them to stop taking the organization seriously when it came to things like meeting report deadlines. Why bother? Being late and negligent actually got someone promoted. The organization sent mixed messages to its employees and was not even aware that they were doing so.

Recognition & Retention

The case of Simon and Dean illustrates the importance of recognition in an organization. One time that I presented *"ACT of Change Management"* to an audience, I asked them how many had left an organization because they felt de-valued or under appreciated.

I was astounded at the number of hands that went up in the room. The response validated research, conducted over the past 60 years, that has continually supported the claim that one of the leading reasons that people leave an organization is a lack of recognition. Interestingly, the leading cause of resignation was *not* salary, as some would likely conclude. In other words, recognition = retention.

Herzberg's Motivation-Hygiene Theory

Frederick Herzberg's (Herzberg et. al., 1959) theory validates this concept, distinguishing as it does between two factors:

1. <u>Motivators (intrinsic factors)</u>

Things that make a job satisfying, e.g., the work itself, recognition, achievement and personal growth

2. <u>Hygiene Factors (extrinsic factors)</u>

Things that do not create positive job satisfaction but the lack of which will create dissatisfaction in a job, e.g., salary, policies and procedures and management techniques

Notice that in Herzberg's model the intrinsic factors are responsible for job satisfaction and that recognition is one of the key factors identified. Conversely, salary is not considered a factor that predicts job satisfaction.

I have always been intrigued by the ritual of the "goodbye party" in organizations. I have often wondered why it takes someone to leave before we appreciate and recognize them. I even speculate that if we had recognized that person before that point, then maybe they would not be leaving in the first place. One organization actually had the opposite practice, which was to throw a celebration when a new employee was hired. Other organizations plan events such as meet and greets and luncheons for new employees. Regardless, the point is well taken: recognition is important in motivating and retaining employees.

Adams' Equity Theory

Further illustrating the importance of recognition, John Stacey Adams (1965) developed equity theory and applied its principles to the workplace.

Equity theory stems from concepts related to relationships, justice and fairness. The main premise of equity theory is that input = output.

With respect to relationships, people experience distress when they perceive inequity; i.e., those who receive too much feel guilt while those who receive too little feel anger. The person then attempts to get rid of their distress by finding ways to restore equity. For example, the worker who is over-recognized may try to overachieve in order to justify the compensation while the under-recognized worker may actually do the opposite and underachieve.

The thinking here is that the under-recognized individual feels that there is no point in working hard because their work is not valued. So they rationalize that they will work at the level at which they are being paid. How many times have we heard colleagues make a statement to the effect of:

"They don't pay me enough to do_____."

People actually become de-motivated, reduce performance and seek change when they perceive that their inputs are not being rewarded. The other outcome for the under-recognized employee is to leave the organization. Thus, we now understand why Simon left his organization. His inputs did not equal his outputs, not to mention the fact that the organization unknowingly robbed him of his job satisfaction by removing his motivation and failing to recognize his performance. However, the story did not end poorly for Simon. Eventually, he found himself working for an employer who did value his performance and recognized his achievements. He ended up in a high-profile management position and his new organization became the beneficiaries of his talents. Eventually, Dean was terminated by the head office due to gross insubordination and spent the rest of his career moving from job to job.

Performance Appraisal: Investment

One of the best ways to recognize and value employees is to make a concerted effort to invest in them. One of the best forums to do so is through performance appraisal. Much has been written on effective ways to engage employee during a performance appraisal. In fact, ACT works exceptionally well when applied to a performance appraisal.

> Be **ASSERTIVE** in addressing issues (performance, conduct or attendance).

> Be **COLLABORATIVE** by coaching the employee to set goals.

> Be **TRANSPARENT** by demonstrating a genuine interest in investing in the employee's success.

To review, here are some sound principles with respect to providing employees feedback in a formal setting:

Do not disclose performance, conduct and attendance issues that have not already been addressed with the employee. There should be no surprises.

Although the formal appraisal may be done yearly, informal appraisals should happen every day between the change leader and employee. We previously discussed the value of "teachable moments" as well as the fact that the change leader must impact the employee at an emotional level in order to promote change.

Giving Feedback Using The Hamburger Method

When giving feedback use the hamburger paragraph method.

> Bun = light conversation focusing on the positive strengths of the employee.

> Meat = the negative or critical issue, phrased in a positive way.

> Bun = light review of discussion and ending on a positive call to action complete with timelines, clear expectations and a plan for the change leader to support and follow up on.

Using this method, the change leader begins with positive information and ends with positive information while putting the critical issue in the centre. How a change leader frames feedback can be critical. If a change leader starts with the negative information first, then it automatically turns the interaction into a negative exchange. Also, if the change leader ends with negative information, then the employee leaves the conversation on a negative note.

The challenge is in how to open the conversation. Even the most challenging employees have something they do well, even if it is just to show up to work. Every change leader must be able to identify things that the employee does well and to articulate it. The change leader then addresses the critical issues and, finally, closes the feedback session by simply reviewing the agreed upon action plan and ending the session on a positive note so that the employee walks away feeling empowered and ready to improve.

Reframing In The Positive

The most challenging part of the Hamburger feedback model is the middle section, in which the critical issues are discussed. In this section, the change leader must find a way to frame a negative issue in the positive. There once was a manager who stated that he would never fire any of his employees. However, he did say that once in a while he would release them to seek other employment opportunities.

This is often not as easy as it sounds; human nature is too immediately focused on the negative before the positive. Negative information comes to mind faster than does positive. A good principle to keep in mind is to focus on problem solving the issue and not castigating the employee; then state the issue (hopefully with some tangible evidence; e.g., some type of written report or official document, policy). The change leader can then illustrate how their behavior or actions are negatively impacting others.

The next step is for the change leader to ask the employee for their feedback. Lastly, collaborate with them and ask them how you can help them improve in the identified area. Often, a change leader can invoke this by using these words:

"How can I support you to improve your (attendance/performance/conduct)? What do you need from me to be successful?"

Below are some examples of "DO's" and "DON'Ts" when it comes to reframing difficult information:

DO Say	DON'T Say
Issue: attendance	
"I have noticed that a recent attendance report shows many occasions of absence or sick days. Can you comment on why this may be occurring?" "Our organization's policy is___ _____. Pattern absenteeism impacts the department by creating more work for others. How can I support you better? What do you need from me to improve in this area?"	"You are always late. What is your explanation for all these absences?"
Issue: performance	
"I have noticed that the work is not being completed in a timely manner. Our practice when it comes to performance is_____. When the work is not completed on time, it affects other departments or clients by _____. How can I support you better? What do you need from me to improve in this area?"	"You are working too slowly. Your co-workers are getting frustrated because we cannot meet deadlines effectively. You must increase your productivity or?"

Issue: conduct (to be discussed further in chapter 8)

Body Language

Body language is also very important. A relaxed posture is more likely to put the employee at ease. A conversational but professional voice tone is appropriate. Location is also important to a good interaction. As discussed in a previous chapter, the change leader's office is typically not recommended, if at all possible, because of what it traditionally represents; i.e., being called in for formal discipline as occurs to a school age child being sent to the principal's office. A lounge or a less formal area may be a better option.

Separating Issues

Separating issues is also highly recommended. Some organizations are pulling issues of attendance and conduct completely out of the formal performance evaluation process. Instead, those organizations deal with each of those issues separately. There are many benefits to this idea. It allows the change leader the opportunity for more on the spot engagement with the employee and to deal with conduct and attendance as it occurs. Also, if employees are aware that there is no disciplinary or attendance issues being addressed at their appraisal, it is more likely to put them at ease. The change leader can then focus more on performance and goal setting.

Time Out/Homework

One of the challenges in this process is the employee who is reluctant or refuses to collaborate. If the change leader makes all the recommendations and sets all the goals, then there will likely be little follow through, as the employee will have no sense of ownership. What should the change leader do when a stalemate is reached with the employee? If the change leader "pushes the envelope" too far then the employee may respond with an aggressive response; this might lead to outright refusal or even a passive aggressive response; e.g., the employee agrees to the action in order to placate the change leader but deliberately does not follow through after the appraisal. In this situation a change leader has reached an impasse and can opt to stop the appraisal or call a recess. The change leader can state to the employee that they have reached a wall and can recommend that they temporarily break and reconvene at a later time. The change leader can set a date to reconvene and give the employee homework. For example, the change leader can then say that between now and the next session, each person will generate five solutions to the issue and bring those to the next session, where they will be discussed until one is mutually agreed upon. What happens if the employee refuses to do so? Then the employee has then chosen to move the issue from performance to conduct, as refusal to comply constitutes insubordination.

Negotiation Theory 101

Perhaps one of the greatest tools in a change leader's repertoire is the power of negotiation. A review of the Thomas Killmann Conflict Model reveals five styles to resolve conflict, based on two axes: assertiveness and cooperation.

Level of Assertiveness	Level of Cooperation	Conflict Style	Outcome
High	Low	Competing	Win-lose
Low	High	Accommodating	Lose-win
Low	Low	Avoiding	Lose-Lose
Moderate	Moderate	Compromise	Win-Lose\Win-Lose
High	High	Collaboration	Win-Win

Source: Thomas-Kilmann Conflict Mode Instrument—also known as the TKI (Mountain View, CA: CPP, Inc, 1974-2009)

The "Competitive" Style

This change leader creates an adversarial relationship. By employing a highly assertive but low cooperation styles, he or she will inevitably conquer the employee; i.e., they will win their position. However, this will ultimately sour the relationship because the conquered employee will feel resentment.

The "Accommodating" Style

This change leader tends to be very passive in communicating the critical issues while being overly cooperative towards the employee

The ACT of Change Management

in an attempt to not offend them. The result is that the employee conquers the change agent, which emboldens the employee and creates resentment from the change agent.

The "Avoiding" Style

This change leader is both non-assertive and non-cooperative. The result is that the key issues are never addressed and the relationship continues to strain further.

The "Compromising" Style

The result is that the change leader gains ground but also loses ground; the employee also gains ground and loses ground.

The "Collaborative" Style

By employing a highly assertive and highly cooperative approach, the change leader gets the commitment to change they need and the employee walks away feeling as though they have lost nothing while having gained something valuable.

Argument Perspective: Needs Versus Wants

To illustrate this point, I am going to tread on a very sensitive issue: differences between men and women. Specifically, I will examine how each gender has its own unique style of communication. After traveling for business for many weeks, I came home one weekend only to have my wife make the following statement: *"You've been away a lot."*

Like the typical male that I am, I naturally answered her back by dealing with her comment at face value. I attempted to justify myself by going into a long explanation about that that was part of my job, that I needed to do this to pay the bills and that I would have time off the road in a few weeks etc. However, I realized that did not appear to appease her dissatisfaction, and I could not understand why. She then made a statement that I responded to with what I believed was a perfectly reasonable and logical response.

However, I learned later that my wife actually had two levels at which she communicated. The first level was on the surface and conveyed what she actually said through the speech and words she used. The second level was deeper and it conveyed what she actually meant. My problem was that I was dealing with the surface level and missing the deeper meaning. So I learned to change my approach. I looked for the feeling behind what she was saying and came to the conclusion that the emotions that were driving her comment were sadness, loneliness and a need for recognition. I had overlooked that while I was away she was doing everything, including taking the kids to school, dealing with illnesses, and managing school, homework and a multitude of household duties.

Once I had that epiphany, I realized that responding to the deeper meaning would be much more effective. So the next time I went away, I arrived home bearing gifts to actively show my appreciation. I also arranged for a babysitter and took her out on a date to a fancy restaurant. This approach worked much better and received a much more favorable response.

We can also look at the two-levels theory and categorize it in terms of:

Level one: Wants (surface)

Level two: Needs (deep)

Putting It Together: Conflict Style & Argument Perspective

An effective change leader must always strive for collaboration, but at times must settle for compromise as the next best option. The change leader who encounters an obstinate employee must be able to use negotiation to break the stalemate. The change leader who collaborates is able to frame things in such a way that both the change leader and the employee gain and neither loses.

Take, for example, Gina, a faithful employee who is struggling with making it to work on time. Upon investigation, it is revealed that Gina has a mother who is receiving treatment for cancer. Gina is her primary caregiver and must take her to the hospital a few days a week to receive treatment first thing in the morning. This will naturally create a conflict with her manager because her lateness has a negative impact on the other employees and the operation.

We can frame the conflict this way, based on what each party wants:

> *Party 1: Gina*
>
> *"I want to be able to take my mother in for her treatments."*
>
> *Party 2: Manager*
>
> *"I want Gina here on time."*

Research in negotiation theory proves that if both conflicted parties deal with the issue at a "wants" level, then it ultimately ends in a power struggle and creates a dynamic called "positional clash." However, if we find a way to reframe the problem in terms of how we can address the needs of party 1 and party 2, then we open up options that were not otherwise obvious.

Framing the argument according to needs makes possible an either/or outcome. Either Gina concedes to what the manager wants or the manager concedes to what Gina wants. Recall, this creates either a win-lose outcome or a lose-win outcome. Chances are that the relationship will also be strained or damaged as a result.

However, if we reframed the argument based on the deeper level, then we could conceptualize it based on what each party actually needs. What does Gina really need in this situation? What does the manager really need in this situation?

> *Party 1: Gina*
>
> *"I need flexibility"*
>
> *Party 2: Manager*
>
> *"I need to ensure the work gets done."*

If we now ask how we can meet both needs, flexibility and getting the work done, then it opens up options. The manager can now sit down with Gina, after reframing the argument, and collaborate with her in order to come up with potential solutions. For example:

> Option #1) Gina could agree to come in later and work later.
>
> Option #2) Gina could do an exchange with a colleague and have them stay late for her and she can then repay the favor.
>
> Option #3) the manager could negotiate to temporarily adjust Gina's schedule to evenings for a time.

Now we have 3 potential options that both parties can agree upon and, in turn, we have increased the likelihood of a win-win result for both individuals. In this instance, a change leader's ability to analyze a conflict and focus on needs, as opposed to wants, provides an opportunity for engagement and collaboration. If such an outcome is reached, then it only can serve to strengthen a change leader's credibility and strengthen the trust between them and the employee.

When it comes to goal setting with an employee, negotiation theory is a must-have skill for every change leader. An environment with the freedom to negotiate can literally change an organization one relationship at a time. It sends the message to the employees that the change leader can be engaged and persuaded on certain issues, if the employee is willing to share the ownership of a problem or issue. This principle literally saved the world during the Cuban missile crisis of 1962, due to the efforts of US President John F. Kennedy.

The Power Of Negotiation: John F Kennedy & The Cuban Missile Crisis Of 1962

Arguably, the most critical event to occur during the cold war between the United States and the Soviet Union occurred in October of 1962. This event also illustrates the power of negotiation as an effective means of dispute resolution.

The ACT of Change Management

Cuban dictator Fidel Castro and Soviet Chairman Nikita Khrushchev conspired to build missile launch sites in Cuba. Missiles in Cuba, situated 90 miles off the US coast, would allow the USSR to have first strike capabilities and to launch nuclear weapons against the eastern seaboard of the US. This situation escalated to the brink of an international nuclear crisis, as Khrushchev deployed an armada of Russian cargo ships to the Caribbean Sea with weapons bound for Cuba. The next series of events would prove to be the defining moment of Kennedy's presidency.

Kennedy's military advisors strongly urged him to immediately attack the Russian ships before they reached Cuba, as well as to plan an invasion of Cuba. However, Kennedy knew that such action would be considered an "act of war" against the Soviet Union, which would undoubtedly retaliate by launching a nuclear attack against the US. The result could have been global nuclear Armageddon. Kennedy came up with an alternate plan that would stop the cargo ships from reaching Cuba, averting a nuclear war. Kennedy imposed quarantine on Cuba and deployed a naval blockade of the Caribbean Sea intended to stop the Russian ships. Such a maneuver was a risk, as the blockade itself could have been viewed as an act of war. However, Kennedy gambled on the fact that Khrushchev would not risk nuclear war over a blockade. The eventual outcome saw Khrushchev ordering the Russian ships to turn back. The end result was a negotiated compromise. Both sides had to concede in order to gain. Russia agreed to remove its missiles from Cuba if the United States agreed to remove theirs from Turkey (which borders Russia).

Kennedy was able to look deeper into the real problem, which was the need to avert a nuclear war, not the power struggle with the Russians for military superiority. By imposing the blockade, Kennedy was able to avoid any armed conflict. Even though Russia ultimately withdrew, neither side suffered any military loss.

Principles Of Financial Investment

In order to goal set and mentor employees, the change leader must be prepared to invest in them. To illustrate, I will draw upon some tips from the business sector on financial goal setting and draw parallels to performance appraisals. Three tips of financial investors include:

Goals—know your goals before you invest.

Market—research the market you wish to invest in.

Time—use it to your advantage, investing early is always the best choice.

If we extend those principles to people in our organization, we can come up with some sound principles for developing potential:

Know Your Goals Before You Invest

The change leader must first create the vision of where he or she needs to go (refer back to chapter 1). If I were to take a trip from New York to Chicago, then the destination determines every action en route. Every highway, turn, rest stop and food stop would be determined by that final destination. This is why it is so important for change leaders to ensure they have a vision and to ensure that they communicate their goals so that their employees can set goals consistent with those of the change leader.

Research The Market

The change leader must know the industry in which they work, including future trends, in order to set a vision. Also, the change leader must know their employees and their potential. Every employee has potential and the challenge of the change leader is to identify that. The only way they can do so is by getting active in the daily work-life of employees and observing how they do their job. Look for areas where they tend to naturally excel and show competence. In the appraisal, make a conscious effort to bring up those positive situations and commend the employee while asking them to find ways that they can become even better at specific skills or tasks.

Use Time To Your Advantage And Invest Early

The change leader must make a concerted effort to capitalize on opportunities in which he or she can engage an employee and do some coaching or give feedback on the spot or shortly after. Especially with new recruits, a change leader should endeavor to give feedback soon after they have had time to observe them in action.

Formal & Informal Recognition

An effective change leader must be able to distinguish between both types of recognition. Formal refers more to official acknowledgements, such as awards, merit, financial bonus and letters of commendation. Informal refers to the everyday positive feedback that the change leader must give to employees. These can be tangible, in the form of gift cards, thank you cards and gifts, or they can be intangible, like spontaneous verbal thanks after a job well done or public praise. Regardless how it is done, it must be presented with sincerity and it must also be specific and identify the accomplishment of the individual, as well as the effect it has had on the organization.

However, recognition does not always come easy to leaders, depending on their personality style. In one example, an employer who was identified as extroverted and task oriented rarely gave his employees positive feedback. The reason he did not give positive feedback was due to his beliefs that:

a) I don't need praise to motivate me to do a good job; therefore, my employees shouldn't need it either.

b) If I give too much praise, it will lead to laziness and non-productivity.

In other words, he managed people according to his own personality instead of learning to adapt to the needs of others, which indicates rigidity. This employer was self-motivated by challenge and mistakenly believed that every employee should be as well. Secondly, I have never heard an employee complain that they were being praised too much. To believe such a concept is absurd, as is the notion that people will stop producing if they receive praise. The opposite is also true: people will complain if they don't receive praise.

Beware Of The "Template"

One of the critical factors of the 60% Status Quo Group is that they can be easily influenced for good by the Change Agents, or for bad by the Instigators and Burnouts. They are ultimately the group that the Change Agents must win over to shift the balance of power. However, sometimes it is possible for the change leader to do everything right when it comes to employee recognition and still be accused of not valuing their employees.

I knew of one change leader who regularly gave out recognition cards and verbal praise at employee meetings, rewarded employee by sending them to education, gave gifts and sent mass emails thanking the team for jobs well done. Yet the majority in this Status Quo Group were persuaded by the negative employee that the manager never gave recognition. The template that was created by the negative employee was "us vs. him." This template was so pervasive that it was ingrained in the minds of the Status Quo employee to the point where even if the change leader gave some type of genuine gift, it was looked upon as suspicious and due to some ulterior motive. That is how powerful a negative template is in an organization. If the template is "he is out to get us," then everything will be seen through that negative lens. So what can a change leader do under these circumstances? The wrong answer would be to give up or stop giving recognition, because that would only serve to reinforce the negative template. The right answer would be to stay the course and continue giving recognition regardless. Eventually, when the culture shifts, those acts of recognition will be remembered and, for some, they will be appreciated. However these employees may be afraid to express this openly because the penalty for endorsing the manager might mean ostracism by the negative employee.

Keith: A Case Study Of Untapped Potential

In chapter four the concept of assessing employee aptitude and achievement was introduced. We learned about the 60% Status Quo group that were categorized by low or untapped aptitude and high achievement. The goal of every change leader is to find or tap into that employee's area of giftedness and develop it. Every employee has certain skills that they do well. An effective change leader will harness that potential to the point where the employee will then move from the 60% Status Quo category into the 20% of Change Agents. The following case study illustrates this concept.

Keith was a shy employee who had worked in the organization for close to 25 years. He was poorly dressed, very soft spoken, inarticulate and appeared to have very low self-confidence. Kevin was the new manager in the organization and Keith was one of his direct reports. Kevin initially put Keith in the lower 20% category of Burnouts (low aptitude & low achievement) because Keith appeared to be an under-achiever and seemed unmotivated in his work. During an audit of employee documentation, Kevin happened to be reviewing some reports written by Keith and, to his surprise, discovered that Keith had remarkable writing abilities. His reports were very thoughtful, articulate and insightful. Astounded, Kevin met with Keith and gave him this feedback. He asked Keith if he would be interested in being a site expert for the computerized client assessment tool that the organization was using. Keith agreed and Kevin sent him to special training, relieving him of his duties so that he could practice and learn the system. Keith did an excellent job with the assessment tool. He began supporting his co-workers in helping to complete their reports. He sent Kevin regular updates, was always accountable and completed his work before the deadlines. Keith's contributions proved to be most helpful in improving operational performance. Keith was lacking in verbal abilities, but tapping into his potential and bringing out his best involved developing his written talents.

This case proves that people are not always what they seem. Even those who we might be quick to "write off" have potential that must be tapped into and developed.

Conclusion: The Great "Undecided"

In the world of politics there is the concept of undecided or "swing voters." These are folks in the general public who hold more moderate and centrist views. Candidates in any political party make a concerted effort to win over this group. Why? Because they can literally swing the momentum to the side of a particular candidate through favorable poll results and an eventual electoral win.

In change management, the Status Quo Group is the group that the change leader must ultimately persuade. The only way he can do this is by empowering the top 20% Change Agents. As illustrated earlier, through positive leadership the top 20% of Change Agents will influence that 60%. Combined, they create an 80% majority inevitably moving towards a positive culture.

Review Of Key Principles

Ultimately, every change leader should make their goal to persuade Status Quo employees to become Change Agents by finding their undiscovered potential and developing their talents and abilities.

Recognition = Retention

Herzberg's Motivational Theory states that recognition is a motivating factor in job satisfaction.

Adams' Equity Theory states that employees become de-motivated and experience poor job satisfaction when they feel their efforts are unrewarded.

Performance appraisal is an opportunity for investment.

Use the hamburger method in giving feedback.

Change leaders need to master the skill of negotiating needs, not wants, to reframe a problem and create positive options.

Change leaders must give both formal and informal recognition.

Change leaders must ultimately win over the 60% Status Quo group by focusing on recognition.

CHAPTER 8

The ACT of Performance Management

In this chapter we deal with a complicated issue that every change leader must face. That is how to performance manage negative employees. Left unchecked, these negative employees will ultimately sabotage positive change. We need not delve into the individual behaviors of negative employees, as every change leader can easily identify and describe them. Instead, we will attempt to understand the psychology, or the "why," behind their behavior in order to find the right strategy to either rehabilitate, neutralize or terminate them. Recall from chapter four that we are referring to the bottom 20% of employees in any organization. We identified these employees as:

Instigators—high aptitude and low achievement

Burnouts—low aptitude and low achievement

The bottom 20% has a powerfully negative influence on the middle 60% of Status Quo employees. So powerful, in fact, that combined they can form a destructive negative 80% coalition. We now know that the strategy of the change leader is to empower the top 20% of Change Agents to swing the momentum towards a positive culture. The negative impact of the bottom 20% has been validated by a poll taken in 2009. 1.5 million workers were asked to rate their level of engagement or feeling of "connectedness" to their organizations. Here were the results:

28% of the workforces are actively (or positively) engaged

55% of the workforces are ambivalently disengaged

> 17% of the workforces are actively (or negatively) disengaged*
>
> (Gallup, 2009)

*That means the bottom 20% are actively working against the change leader. To make matters worse, negative employees refuse to:

- Take ownership of their behavior
- Make efforts to improve their situation
- Leave.

So why do they stay? Why do they continue to work in a place where they are unhappy and make others miserable? What exactly do they want? The answer is: no one really knows, and neither do they. The fact is that most of the negative employee haven't thought about things that deeply because it requires two things:

a) Honest reflection
b) A decision

Both are critical things they refuse to do. I would argue that the strategy of every change leader is to force the negative employee into a position that forces them to pick a) or b).

Leadership As A Reflective Practice

Most negative employees refuse to reflect upon their own practice, or they are incapable of doing so. To take a look at one's own faults and brokenness is difficult and painful to do. It is far easier to avoid introspection. Contrast that with positive employees who engage in reflection on a daily basis. Reflection simply means to look back on one's actions, interactions and performance regularly and to determine ways to improve. To get negative employees to engage in honest reflection is perhaps the most difficult thing a change leader can do. Few will actually succeed at this; however, those who manage to do so have a solid chance at rehabilitating a negative employee. Rehabilitating a negative employee is the first priority for the change leader.

Not To Decide Is To Decide

Equally difficult and unlikely is for negative employees to actually motivate themselves to do something about their problems. Indecision is far easier than decision. So, in effect, to refuse to decide is actually a decision. The person has actually chosen to accept their situation; the caveat is that they intend to make sure you and everyone else never forget it.

Quit Your Job

In my early years as a speaker I would typically find myself in situations where there were some negative employees who were in attendance at my presentation. They would typically present to me impossible scenarios that illustrated that they were unhappy with their boss or co-workers. In an attempt to keep a positive tone, I would try to get them to find options and to problem solve. Every scenario I gave them was met with either mocking or a comment that the solution was unrealistic. As time went on I grew tired of these impossible scenarios, and one day a negative employee challenged me. This time I employed a more direct approach. I told her to quit her job. I went on to ask her: "who is putting a gun to your head to work here? If you are unhappy there are many other jobs in the world." I went on to say that she had presented me with a no-win situation, and the only thing to do in those circumstances was to cut her losses and leave the organization.

You could have heard a pin drop in the room. In fact, the employee's manager was standing at the back of the room and if there were a thought balloon above her it would have read, "I can't believe he just said that." The negative employee who asked the question stood there speechless and eventually sat down. Others in the audience actually nodded their heads in support of my statement. I believe I was able to get that negative employee to do a) and reflect. However, when the seminar evaluations came back her comment read: "why does it always have to come back to employee having to resign?" Her comment went on to blame the management, which meant that she refused to do b) and make a healthy decision on her own.

In The Wrong Line Of Work

Have you ever experienced poor customer service from a rude employee? Almost everyone has at one point in his or her life. Why is it that in many of the helping professionals, like teaching and nursing for example, there always has to be one miserable and nasty person working in a given organization? You would think that only benevolent people would gravitate to those jobs, but sometimes the opposite is true. The question to ponder is whether or not these folks are aware that they are rude and negative. The answer is obvious. Most don't believe that they are negative. Again, this could be for the reasons we just discussed: the lack of capacity for honest reflection. I remember a manager trying to complete a performance appraisal with an employee who was well known to be lazy and have a nasty disposition towards her colleagues. Part of the appraisal involved the employee rating her own skills. When she and the change leader sat down to review the appraisal, the employee over-rated herself in almost every category. She saw herself as personable, easy to work with and productive. The manager then asked her for evidence of her high rating and she gave very weak examples, but was nonetheless convinced that she was a stellar employee by virtue of the fact that she had worked there for over 25 years. Every attempt the change leader made to get the employee to challenge her own perceptions was futile. She would not be convinced otherwise.

However, there are others who are aware that they are negative but who just don't care. Some of these employees have the attitude that the work is a simple paycheck, that it would be too difficult to change jobs and that they are comfortable where they are. Many of these individuals are longstanding employees who have seen many turnovers in management, so they tend to entrench themselves in order to wait out the change leader. I remember one organization in which the employees were actually proud of the reputation that they were able to run every manager "out of town."

Profiling The Problem Employee

A worthwhile exercise for any group of change leaders is to actually analyze what makes up a negative employee. The **problem employee profile** is a hypothetical construct. The change leaders in an organization should actually work together to create this profile and then discuss the results and what it means for the organization.

THE PROBLEM EMPLOYEE PROFILE

Based on a format developed by Ryan, D. & Marlowe, B. (2004). Used with permission.

Part A: Demographic Information

- Age
- Gender
- Specific department where they work
- Years of service
- Work history
- Education level
- Problem behavior list
- Personal problems

Part B: Current Performance Management Strategy

- What we have been doing in an attempt to manage this employee?
- Results of performance appraisals
- Effectiveness of discipline taken
- Impact on department
- What is working and what is not working

Part C: "Perfect World" Performance Management Strategy

- If we had all the tools, money and resources we needed, how would we performance manage this employee? Make a wish list.

Part D: Identified Gaps

If we compare Part B with Part C, we see there are gaps we can identify with respect to the following issues not being addressed:

- Service provision
- Education
- Resources

Discussion

1. What common themes emerged from different groups?

2. What standards are either missing or not being enforced that would help to hold this person more accountable?

3. What actions items based on gaps can be used moving forward?

<u>Analysis</u>

In the seminar I usually do this as a small group exercise. Each group gets a flipchart and marker and records, then reports their finding back to the larger group. What is interesting is that in almost every case, the majority of participants end up creating the same profile.

Usually this is the typically profile:

- Female (I do not dare provide commentary here but female is always the most common gender chosen)
- Middle-aged
- Many years of service, usually between 15-25 years
- Union shop steward
- History of bad attitudes, insubordination, passive aggressiveness and defiance of management
- Ring leader and bully of peers
- Has domestic or personal problems at home
- Suspected to have a mental illness such as personality disorder
- Issues with absenteeism
- All attempts to performance manage have been unsuccessful
- Employee knows how to beat the system; does damage but knows to cover their tracks
- This one employee is so toxic that they are bringing the whole team of employees down

- This employee lacks the capacity for self-reflection and does not see themselves as negative
- They refuse to leave the organization

Positive Spin: Can Problem Employees Be Useful?

<u>Gap Assessment</u>

Problem employees can be useful in determining gaps that need to be addressed by the organization. The problems created by negative employees often reveal failure or the absence of critical organizational policies. Using the "Problem Employee Profile," change leaders can identify gaps and develop ways to improve practices and performance. Below is a list of issues that is typically generated by participants in the seminar when the Problem Employee Profile has been used:

> *Absenteeism & Attendance*—A chronic problem in every organization and common too many negative employees. Many are non-engaged and they feel no loyalty or obligation to the organization, which in turn entitles them to take time off whenever they choose. There is no difference between sick days and vacation days. The cost associated with absenteeism can be crippling to many organizations.
>
> *Code Of Conduct & Anti-Bullying Policies*—If there is no standard for conduct, then a change leader has nothing that can hold negative employee to account. In today's age of technology, organizations must look seriously at issues, such as social networking and cyber bullying, that did not exist a decade ago.
>
> *Rules Of Scheduling & Overtime*—Issues of worker fatigue can be detrimental and even dangerous in many industries, particularly health and human services.
>
> *Recruitment & Orientation*—This involves ensuring that there are screening practices that recruit the right individuals to the organization. Also, if the change leader was to look back on the career of the negative employee, it is likely that their behavior

was somehow enabled either by a previous leader who was non-assertive or because there was no specific policy that identified their behavior as unacceptable. Proper orientation to standards is crucial in getting new recruits off on the right foot by detailing negative behavior from the onset.

Negative Employee As A Barometer

An old cliché states that with every crisis means opportunity as well as upheaval. The same can be applied to the negative employee. If the change leader is stuck with them, then he or she might as well use them for something productive, such as a barometer for assessing the current culture.

A change leader can assess the type of culture in their workplace by examining the power, scope and impact of the most negative instigator. To illustrate, in a negative and entitled culture, the most negative instigator will typically be visibly prominent. When they have the benefit of power on their side, they won't hesitate to flaunt it. Their presence is almost like the schoolyard bully prowling around looking for victims and ensuring that other students know they are there and so to stay in line. They physically impose themselves in almost every situation. If there is a discussion to be had, they will facilitate it. If there is an employee who steps out of line and violates the unspoken culture laws (discussed in chapter 5), the instigator and their minions will be there to punish them. If the change leader attempts to introduce a new idea or project, they will either be the first to verbally disagree or will covertly defy it.

However, when the culture begins to shift, the opposite is also true. The bully-instigator will be less prominent as they will have a decreased number of followers. The more the culture shifts and the more the change leader raises the bar of conduct and performance, the more the bully will stand out.

Negative employees can also be a barometer to help the change leader assess their own effectiveness. It is a common temptation for every change leader to want to be liked by everyone. It is also understandably difficult and de-moralizing to be unpopular with all one's employees. However, the change leader must assess which group is acting in opposition to their leadership. If the change leader is unpopular with the bottom 20% of negative employees, then that usually means they are doing their job correctly.

The opposite is also true: if the change leader is popular with the bottom 20% of negative employees, then that usually means they are not doing their job correctly. This is a common pitfall for many in leadership. It is far easier to change processes without showing the courage to take the hits involved with changing the culture. Culture change happens one employee at a time and involves personal and professional risk for the change leader. As we discovered in earlier chapters, few will take that journey.

Declaration Of War

Justice is the foundation of good governance and the politics of appeasement have no place in the process of change. As much as we want to avoid unnecessary conflict at all costs, we must first be prepared to take a moral stand against those behaviors that are ultimately destructive to the organization. This is where the change leader will make his or her ultimate stand. In essence, this means to draw a line in the sand and say to those engaged in negative behaviors that they will go no further, that their behavior is unacceptable and that it will no longer be tolerated.

After all, isn't a change leader also supposed to be diplomatic and in pursuit of peace and harmony in the organization? The answer is an unequivocal "yes." However, before the change leader can work towards peace, he or she must be prepared to declare war on issues like misconduct, malpractice, bullying, coercion and harassment.

If this concept is difficult to digest, then consider it from the point of view of the negative employee's victims: the 60% Status Quo and the 20% Change Agents. The latter employees are looking to the change leader to restore justice to the organization. Left unchecked, the negative employee will recruit the 60% and sway them into poor performance. Also, the negative 20% will attack the top 20% of Change Agents, because they are a direct threat to their power and influence. The change leader must be prepared to declare war on the bottom 20% in an effort to protect the top 20% of

Change Agents, because without them the change leader cannot move the organization forward.

Case Study: Marnie and Cora Part I

Cora was a longstanding employee who had been at the organization for over 10 years when Marnie arrived. Marnie was young and aspiring, full of great ideas and positive energy. Cora was the known bully in the department who no one dared to cross. Before long, Marnie found herself in the cross hairs of Cora when a position for assistant manager was posted. Marnie had less experience than Cora but regularly exceeded her in performance and achievement. Marnie applied for the assistant manager position and was successful. Cora responded by beginning a campaign to smear Marnie's reputation by turning the other employees against her. Gossip began to brew behind the scenes. Marnie would come in to work only to find that Cora had sabotaged many of the new projects and processes that she had put in place. The manager at the time was actually intimidated by Cora and did little to protect Marnie, all in an attempt to keep the peace in the department. The bullying towards Marnie intensified over the next year and Marnie's health began to suffer due to the stress; she also became bitter towards the manager for his inability to deal with Cora. Cora not only ruined Marnie, but she also subjugated the manager: it clearly became known to all that Cora ran the department and did whatever she wanted with impunity.

During Cora's reign of terror, allegations of customer abuse skyrocketed, absenteeism was the highest that it had ever been, and operational efficiency was among the lowest in the organization. Employee morale was at rock bottom and the department had the worst reputation in the organization, which affected recruiting. Eventually the manager of the department was fired and Marnie eventually left on a sick leave. Cora had won . . . . or so she thought.

Fortunately, the story does not end there. However, this case illustrates that there are consequences for the change leader when he or she refuses to ACT when it comes to dealing with negativity head on. The manager in this story attempted to be diplomatic with a pathological employee who accepted no responsibility or ownership for her own behavior. This is a wakeup call to those change leaders who refuse to declare war on destructive behavior: you must consider that the cost of passivity on their change agent employees and even your own careers.

Psychopathology Of Negative Employees

In the story above, Cora began a campaign to smear Marnie's reputation and sabotage her work. In order to be successful she had to find weak-minded recruits, or lieutenants, to do her bidding for her. They were the ones who swore loyalty to her; and even when she was not on shift they continued her dirty work on her behalf.

Bullies travel in packs because there is strength in numbers. A lion versus a single hyena is no contest. Most bullies are not foolish enough to take on the change leader's authority one on one, as it would create obvious grounds to claim insubordination. Instead, they take a more stealth approach. Just as a solitary lion versus a pack of hyenas is a dreadful mismatch, a change leader facing off against a bully and the collective strength of an accompanying gang is not a favorable contest for the leader. The change leader must be aware of when he or she is being baited into a situation in which the bully has the numbers advantage. However, what is it that motivates and organizes these negative employees and their followers? We will examine five concepts that may help us to understand them better.

> *Stockholm Syndrome*—Named after a famous hostage-taking crisis in 1973 at a bank in Stockholm, Sweden, this describes the paradoxical phenomena of captives sympathizing with their captors. To apply this concept to our discussion, it is easier for the 60% of Status Quo employees to join the instigating bully and sympathize with their cause than it is to stand against them and risk ostracism.

> *Victim Mentality*—One of the hallmarks of victimhood is the assignment of blame on others for things that happen in the world of the victim. Victims create other victims; one can see how easy it is to win recruits sympathetic to the victims' cause by convincing others of how poorly they are treated and to, in turn, arouse anger and resentment towards those in authority. Personally I have found this pervasive in many labor groups and unions. Their platform is

often that of playing to the anger and misery of others, instead of encouraging positivity and constructive thinking. I have also noticed that when a change leader is finally able to bring a negative employee to justice, the negative employee suddenly reverts to being a victim, after they are exposed. I find it ironic that these people who have made careers out of victimizing others break down into tears when faced with severe discipline or termination. I often wished that the employees who were legitimate victims of this person could see the instigator-bully in this light.

Mob Mentality—This appears to be the next logical step after the instigator-bully has successfully convinced the masses that they are victims. Also termed "herd mentality," the theory behind this holds that people attempt to assimilate the behaviors and habits of the group with whom they are surrounded. Therefore, if victimization and abuse are established as the norm, then the "herd" of Status Quo employees will inevitably join in the behavior; this is similar to the behavior of an angry lynch mob.

Contagion Theory—Related to mob mentality, this theory, drawn from social psychology, holds that people who are in a crowd act differently towards people than those who are thinking individually. The perception of anonymity provided by the group often allows average people, such as those in the middle 60% Status Quo group, to do horrendous acts that they would not otherwise do if acting individually.

Ego Defense Mechanisms- Sigmund Freud, the founder of psychoanalytic theory, postulated the concept of the subconscious, which is the part of our mind that operates according to unconscious mental processes. Simply put, we repress things like guilt, anxiety and shame and attempt to cope with these by avoiding them. I will apply these techniques to the bully, and they include: passive aggression, denial of one's own behavior and the projection of hostility towards the change leader.

Understanding the psychological make-up of negative employees provides the change leader with the advantage of knowing their adversary better.

Knowing them better, as an opponent, allows the change leader to employ the right strategy to hold them accountable for their behavior.

Bullies operate by alienating those who challenge or oppose their views. In essence, the change leader must employ the same tactic, alienating the bully by taking out their power base—their minions or the lieutenants who are subordinates to the bully—by using performance management. By neutralizing that group, the bully's base of support will be weakened. This, in turn, will help the change leader isolate the bully.

Sun Tzu & The Art Of Performance Management

"Know your adversary and know yourself and you will always be victorious."

Sun Tzu

Regarded as the most brilliant military scientist and strategist who ever lived, General Sun Tzu's teachings are renowned the world over and have been studied by some of history's greatest military leaders, like Napoleon and Eisenhower. His principles on warfare are also applicable to our discussions on performance management. Listed in the chart below are some of Sun Tzu's principles, along with some thoughts on how they can be used to hold negative employees accountable for their behavior.

Sun Tzu's Principles	*Applications*
1. It is always better to win without having to fight	*If a change leader can persuade a negative employee to change their behavior of their own volitions, it is a victory and is preferable to having to performance manage.*
2. Expediency is the key in victory.	
3. Avoid protracted campaigns that strain resources.	*Investigations for poor conduct must be acted on immediately and disciplined swiftly.*
4. A good commander never attacks out of anger or rage.	

5. If you are not in danger do not start a war.	Drawn out performance management strains resources, lowers morale and allows negative employees to entrench themselves.
6. Never attack the adversary who is keen and full of spirit.	
7. Attack the adversary when he is confused and unprepared and worn down mentally.	Check your emotions and act of out rationality and objectivity.
8. Beware when being baited by the adversary.	Use discretion and pick your battles. Know what issues to ACT on and when not to ACT.
9. Always stay on offense and not on defense.	It is best to confront negative employees when they are on their own, to prevent the audience effect.
10. Always fight the battle on your terms and not your adversary's.	Use the element of surprise to your advantage and confront them when they are not expecting it, so they do not have time to prepare a defense.
11. Always take the position of higher ground.	
12. Never underestimate the adversary.	Know when negative employees are deliberately trying to trip you up. Anticipate it and out maneuver them.
13. Watch out for the places where spies might hide.	Push your agenda forward continuously and don't give negative employees time to time to plot sabotage.
14. Intelligence gathering is important to victory.	
15. Wise planning = victory.	Never allow negative employee to take control of an interaction because this creates a power struggle and damages your credibility.
16. Focus on giving troops energy and momentum.	
17. Unite troops in purpose.	

The ACT of Change Management

18. Sometimes putting the troops in a desperate circumstances bring out their best performance. 19. A victorious commander is one who changes plans to suit the circumstances. 20. 5 Fatal flaws of a commander: • Reckless • Cowardly • Quick-tempered • Easily offended • Too compassionate	*Never resort to underhanded or unethical tactics to performance manage negative employee.* *Underestimating negative employees gives them the element of surprise.* *Beware the lieutenants and minions of the instigator-bully and the damage they can cause.* *Always anticipate and observe the negative employee's potential countermoves meant to sway momentum back in their favor.* *Use experienced advisors to help guide you.* *Build morale with your Change Agents.* *Help your Change Agents buy into a shared vision* *Don't be too quick to rescue your Change Agents, as adversity forces them to problem solve and find solutions to impossible situations.* *Always change the playbook to keep the negative employee on their toes and avoid being too predictable.* *Excessive risk taking can be disastrous.* *Fear of negative employees cripples the change leader.*

	Over reacting causes reckless reactions. *Being over sensitive to criticism and personal attacks makes you an easy target.* *Beware of being too lenient with negative employees, it may come back to haunt you. Sometimes you have to make an example of them.*

Principles & Goals Of Performance Management

Performance Management:

- Is solutions focused.

- Focuses on closing the gap between actual performance and desired performance.

- Requires the **ACT** principle to be applied.

- Is intended to be restorative not punitive.

- Is based on measureable standards.

There are three main outcomes when it comes to confronting negative employee about their behavior:

1. Rehabilitate
2. Neutralize
3. Terminate

<u>Rehabilitate</u>

Defined, it means to coach and collaborate with them to change their own behavior. This is the absolute best outcome and should be the first goal of every performance management attempt by a change leader. Just as a change leader must not rush into discipline, he or she must give the negative employee an opportunity to change. A change leader is not responsible for the decisions made by the employees. However, the change leader is responsible for the environment in which they make those decisions.

The change leader must create an environment of learning, growth and recovery. What could be a more positive morale booster than for employees to see a negative peer improve their behavior and conduct? Such an achievement would gain tremendous credibility for the change leader (refer back to chapter 7 on principles of coaching).

Solution-Focused Dialogue - The principles of Solutions Focused Brief Therapy (SFBT) provide a powerful interviewing technique used to aid the change leader in coaching negative employee. They are based on the work of Milton Erickson and In Soo Kim Berg (1994). This counseling technique is different than insight-oriented psychotherapy, as it is pragmatic and focuses on empowering people to find solutions, not finding out why people behave the way they do. The change leader can ask specific questions based on the employee's ability to self-reflect and take ownership for wanting to change. The questions below provide a template to assist you in developing a solutions-focused dialogue.

1) Think about your own behavior and identify something that you do that you don't like doing and would like to change.

2) How open are you to changing that behavior? (check one)

- ❑ *Not open at all*
- ❑ *Somewhat open*
- ❑ *Completely open*

3) "If you were to go to bed tonight and a miracle happened where your problem would be solved......" (The Miracle Question)

- a. *What would be different?*
- b. *How would you be different?*
- c. *How would others react or be able to notice a difference?*

4) Can you think of a time when you had success with changing that behavior/situation? What did you do that might have worked in that situation? (Exception to the Rule)

5) What small step could you take today that might improve the problem? (Small Steps)

6) If you were to achieve success with this "small step," do you think it might increase your confidence and motivate you to make more changes in the future? (Ripple Effect)

Neutralize

There are some negative employees who are affected by a toxic environment. Even though a change leader cannot directly change people, they can change the environment. Sometimes there are negative employees who don't need to be directly confronted because it is clear that they are collateral damage of the true Instigators and bullies. Shifting the momentum to positive can move them from the bottom 20% to the middle 60%, which is still an improvement. To get them to stop complaining and do their work with a good attitude consistently is a both a realistic goal and a win. This may happen automatically, as the culture changes one person at a time, or it may happen due to the increased influence of Change Agents (see chapter 6).

To Terminate Or Not To Terminate?

The traditional process of formal discipline usually includes 5 steps:

1. Informal chat or coaching conversation to bring the issue to the employee in a spirit of restoration.
2. Verbal warning
3. Written warning
4. Suspension
5. Termination

If the change leader provides the right environment, including giving the troubled employee all the necessary resources and supports to improve their own performance and conduct, and they still refuse, then the employee has fired him or herself.

The Tragic Reality Of Terminations

Much has been written on ways to investigate, document and terminate employees. This must be the last resort, and the burden of proof is on the change leader to demonstrate that they have used all resources to try to rehabilitate the employee, without success. Termination is, in essence, a statement that the employee would be a risk and liability to the organization if they continued to be employed there. In non-unionized environments, terminating with cause is much easier when compared to unionized environments, where problem employees often benefit from protection and a labor management process that tends to benefit the employee.

The reality in some unionized environments is that there are horror stories of change leaders who have followed the correct performance management process, to the letter, and were able to prove employee incompetence or misconduct, but had to settle in a mediation or arbitration process. Reasons for this may include the fact that the employee has been with the organization for many years but never had any issues identified in previous performance appraisals. I personally have witnessed, on more than one occasion, an instance in which an arbitrator has ruled that an organization had prematurely terminated the employee and has actually recommended that they be given their job back, in spite of gross negligence and incompetence. Imagine the damage caused if that employee returned to the workplace. They would be entrenched and be virtually untouchable. Any attempts by the change leader to performance manage after that point would be seen as a reprisal against the employee and would be subject to a harassment charge. In some cases, the organization must bite the bullet and offer some type of pay out package to get the employee to leave voluntarily. Some would find it a moral outrage to actually reward an employee for bad behavior, but it may be the lesser of two evils if, indeed, the employee is that much of a risk, particularly in the health and human services field. The reality is that, in some extreme examples, the change leader can do everything right in terms of the process of investigation and documentation and still not be able to terminate the problem employee.

Case Study: Marnie and Cora Part II

After Marnie left on stress leave and the department manager was let go, the organization hired another manager, Stephanie. Stephanie was different than her predecessor. She employed the principles of ACT. She was assertive in calling out bad behavior and setting limits on poor performance. She applied principles of collaboration and coached her employees, educating them on the organization's code of conduct, and made herself available to solve problems as they occurred. She also made herself transparent by stating that she would hold everyone to the same standard that she held herself. She was consistent in the way she followed up with employees, which was a direct challenge to Cora, who tried to convince everyone that Stephanie played favorites. At times, Cora would directly challenge Stephanie's authority in front of other employees who watched to see how Stephanie would react. Stephanie was careful to not allow Cora to invoke an emotional reaction in her, but she never backed down from a confrontation. When she sensed Cora escalating, she took control of the interaction and literally escorted Cora out of the room to a private spot, where she held her accountable for her behavior.

Stephanie recognized that Cora did have leadership potential and even offered her an opportunity of advancement, if she would be willing to work with Stephanie to improve her performance. Stephanie agreed to invest in Cora by sending her to workshops and courses, if she would be willing to set goals and allow Stephanie to coach her towards the promotion. However, Cora took offense to Stephanie's offer, as she believed she did not need to be coached and that she should automatically get the promotion due to her years of experience.

Soon, the employees began coming to Stephanie to report Cora and her bad behavior, which was something that no one dared do in the past. They took the risk because they felt protected by Stephanie, who had proven that she was a person of her word, and because she continually reminded them of their obligation to positive employee conduct. Productivity improved, absenteeism declined and morale steadily grew. Soon Cora's antics stood out as unacceptable, and the employees began to tune her out when she started to rant and rave about her grievances with management. Stephanie managed to put pressure on Cora, investigating her on two different occasions, for abuse towards clients and negligence of duty. Cora, unable to cope with the pressure put on her from Stephanie, went on sick leave for several months. During those months of Cora's absence, morale in the department improved significantly.

Realizing that Stephanie was not going to back off her pursuit, and that she was losing her power base, Cora returned from sick leave and promptly applied for a transfer out of the department. Stephanie wisely forwarded all of her documentation to the new manager, who wound up suspending Cora for abusive behavior less than a year after her transfer.

Recall that the strategy of every change leader is to force the negative employee into a position that forces them to either honestly reflect or make a decision. Stephanie was able to put Cora into a position that forced her to look at herself and make a decision about her future. Stephanie's success in this case study can be attributed to her ability to use ACT to inform her practice as a change leader by using many of the key concepts in this chapter, as summarized below.

Review Of Key Principles

Negative employees consist of people like Burnouts and Instigators.

In most organizations, 17% of employees are actively disengaged and working against the employer.

A change leader must force negative employees to engage in self-reflection and decision-making.

Negative employees can serve a positive purpose, as demonstrated by the Problem Employee Profile, which is used to identify organizational gaps.

Negative employees can also serve a positive purpose by acting as a barometer for the organization and change leader.

Change leaders must be prepared to declare war on negative and destructive behaviors.

Negative employees and their minions can be understood using psychological concepts such as The Stockholm Syndrome, victim mentality, mob mentality, contagion theory and psychodynamic ego defense mechanisms.

The principles of Sun Tzu can prove useful in guiding a change leader towards holding negative employees accountable for their conduct and behavior.

Performance management is designed to be restorative in nature.

Principles of Solutions Focused Brief Therapy can be helpful in coaching negative employees who are able to engage in self-reflection and are willing to take ownership of their behavior.

Some negative employees can be neutralized without active performance management.

A change leader is not responsible for the decisions made by employees, but they are responsible for the environment in which the employees make decisions.

Termination should be the last resort; this should occur when employees have basically fired themselves.

The burden of proof for termination falls on the change leader, so documentation is critical.

Even though a change leader may follow the process of performance management precisely, that may not guarantee a termination in some extreme cases.

CHAPTER 9

MAKING THE CASE FOR ACT

To review the change journey thus far. The ACT model of change management entails the following 5 step process:

Component 1) Integrate ACT Into You, As The Change Leader.

Component 2) Assess Your Individual Employees By Looking At Achievement And Aptitude.

Component 3) Assess Your Organization's Culture.

Component 4) Influence Employee Behavior To Create A Culture Of Achievement.

Component 5) Empower, Recognize And Performance Manage Employees

MDM: ACT MODEL OF CHANGE MANAGEMENT

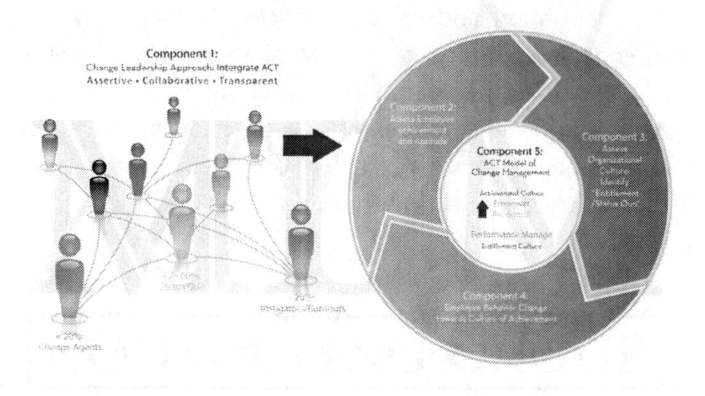

Assertive • Collaborative • Transparent

Many concepts have been introduced and illustrated over the past 8 chapters. In order to consolidate and apply this information, two case studies will be presented. The first case study provides an example of a leader who empowered the top 20% of Change Agents, which created positive momentum towards change. The second case study addresses a unique situation in which empowering the top 20% was not feasible and the successful method utilized a two-pronged approach, which included empowering the top 20% of Change Agents while simultaneously performance managing the bottom 20% of Instigators and Burnouts.

Case Study Organization A: Empowering The Change Agents

In organization A, the employee culture had the typical features of entitlement. Many of the employees could be described as:

- Insubordinate
- Un-teachable
- Mistrustful of management
- Refusing to accept change
- De-skilled and performing far below the industry standard
- Frequently absent and sick from work
- Bullied by one dominant instigator who was known to be abusive towards co-workers and clients

This group of employees did not hesitate to tell people what they thought about the organization and its new policies. In fact, they were often characterized as "in your face" or somewhat aggressive in their approach to the leadership. The other feature of this culture was that they were very close with one another and frequently looked out for each other. This group could also have been characterized by "groupthink." In other words, what one felt they all experienced. When one of them spoke or complained it was on behalf of all of them.

They fit the aforementioned template of "management is out to get us," and actually...they were right. Appearances were deceiving, because a deeper look into this history of this group revealed that they had recently endured the experience of an autocratic department manager who was characterized as heavy handed and abusive. It is no small wonder that this group huddled around one another and became emotionally close, because this served as a protective mechanism for them.

What is not obvious in this example is that, despite this, there were many positives that could be used and developed to build positive change. For example:

- Their tendency to speak their mind also meant they could express themselves and they could be engaged.
- They never claimed to be better than they were, which meant that they were teachable and open to feedback.
- They protected one another, which meant they had empathy and compassion.
- They used groupthink, which meant if one could be positively swayed then all could be positively swayed.

The ability to see opportunity in crisis and turn disadvantage into advantage is the mark of an effective change leader.

Using the ACT model the, change leader began the process:

<u>Component 1) Integrate ACT Into You, As The Change Leader.</u>

One of the first acts of business for the change leader was to hold an employee meeting and state her approach to management:

Assertive, meaning she tackled issues directly with her employee.

Collaborative, which meant she worked with her employee to solve problems.

Transparent, which meant she had no hidden agenda.

She also made it clear that she, in turn, expected her employees to use the same approach with her, by using ACT. She not only stated this openly, she lived by these principles every day and set the example.

Component 2) Assess Individual Employee's Achievement and Aptitude

Her next step was to complete a personnel review over time using the achievement and aptitude criteria. Her assessment revealed that only 10% of the employees were top achievers and Change Agents, 66% were Status Quo and 23% were negative Instigators and Burnouts.

Component 3) Assess Organizational Culture

The negative 23% clearly had a stranglehold and, combined with the 66% of Status Quo, created an almost 90% downward shift towards entitlement, which explained the toxic culture she was seeing.

Components 4) & 5) Influence Employee Behavior Change To Create A Culture Of Achievement /Empower, Recognize And Performance Manage

The change leader began to meet regularly with the top 10% of Change Agents. She set goals, earned their trust, supported them, sent them for external education on leadership and met with them regularly for coaching sessions. She also focused on recruiting and changed the interview templates to reflect what she felt were the necessary criteria of the employees that she wanted. As a result she added more high achievement and high aptitude Change Agents to her team.

The positive impact of the Change Agents influenced the Status Quo and many of them also began to improve their performance and move into the top-achieving category. In fact, through careful recruiting and improving the Status Quo, she was able to grow the top Change Agents from 10%, in the first year, to 38% in the second year.

As the culture shifted, the tipping point came when the team decided that they had had enough of the dominant instigator and bully in the unit. Collectively, they expelled that individual, who was forced to transfer out. The number of negative employees decreased in one year for two reasons:

1) The negative employees realized that they were losing power and they could not intimidate the change leader.

2) Some of the negative employees who were low performance and low potential actually improved their performance and moved into the Status Quo category.

After the first year, the negative employees dropped from 23% to 9%, and by year three they were less than 3%. The results of this change leader's journey can be seen below in the table.

Table 1: Organization A

	Spring Year 1	**Spring Year 2**	**Spring Year 3**
+ Change Agents	**10%**	**38%**	**34%**
+/- Status Quo	**66%**	**53%**	**63%**
- Instigators/ Burnouts	**23%**	**9%**	**3%**

According to graph 1 (below), Spring Year 1 illustrates a negative skew, indicating a negative entitlement culture. Spring Year 2 and 3 illustrates a positive skew, indicating a shift to more positive culture. One can clearly see that investing in the top achieving Change Agents paid dividends in this example. By the end of year three, there was almost a complete reversal. Year one saw a 90% downward shift. In contrast, year 3 showed a dramatic 97% upward shift.

Graph 1: Organization A

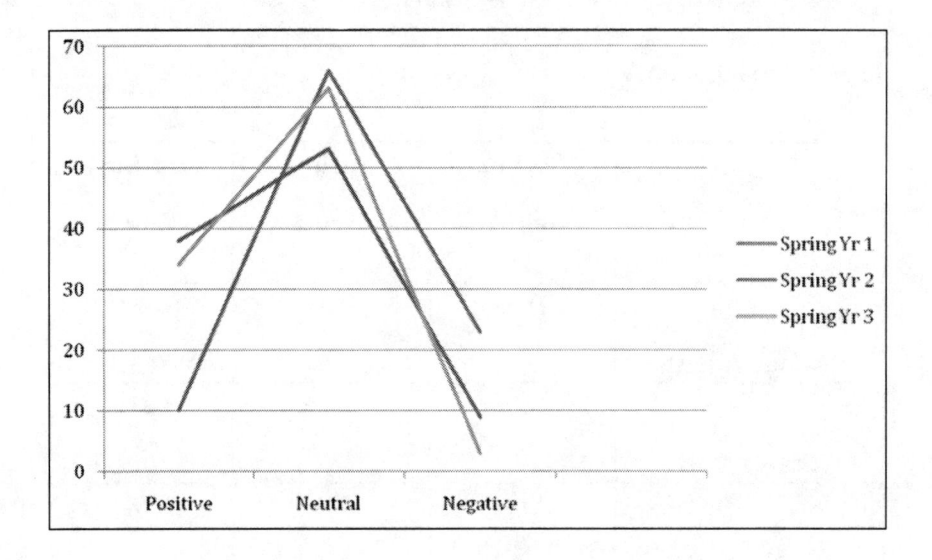

In the space of less than three years, Organization A went from a culture of entitlement to a culture of achievement, as evidenced by:

- Higher employee retention
- Lower employee turnover
- Increased recruiting
- Improved reputation
- Increased innovation leading to higher performance and productivity
- Decreased absenteeism and sick time
- Increase in the number of employees asking for education and upgrading their skills
- Improved morale

Sun Tzu principle:
"Use normal force in daily battle but use extraordinary force to win."

As we saw in the previous chapter, sometimes the change leader can do everything right and still lose in the arena of labor management. Recall that the burden of proof is always on the employer and that sometimes even the most negative of employee are not easy to rehabilitate, neutralize or even terminate.

We also saw in chapter 6 that empowering the top 20% of Change Agents typically creates the critical mass required to tip an organization towards positive change (Gladwell. 2002). However, what happens when the change leader is not able to successfully empower the top 20%? What happens if the culture is so negative and so entitled that what is required is to virtually performance manage everyone? The answer is a concept called "blitz remediation."

Blitz Remediation: Mass Performance Management

Intense organizational problems sometimes warrant an urgent and intense process of mass performance management. At times there are extraordinary circumstances that create the need to concentrate all available administrative and educational resources on a particular area within an organization in an effort to force the environment to tip in a favorable direction. Such circumstances could be excessive consumer complaints, as well as extremely toxic work environments that carry serious legal and safety implications. In situations such as these, the management of the organization cannot afford to wait for the gradual process of change to occur, but must act immediately.

Blitz remediation involves the leadership team focusing all resources either on one department at a time, or on one issue at a time, e.g., attendance, bullying and harassment. The benefits of using such approach include:

- A time sensitive rapid approach.
- Builds solidarity and cohesiveness among the leadership team.
- Creates a consistent leadership approach.
- Sends a strong message of unity among the leadership team to employees.

- Increased leadership presence often reveals and exposes poor performance and conduct.
- Increased leadership presence provides opportunity for the change leader to deal with challenges head on, and when they occur.
- Leadership team members mutually support each other.

As much as there are benefits, there are always drawbacks to using this approach; these include:

- Concentrating resources in one area often means other areas may suffer from a lack of supervision or support.
- Many organizations that are smaller and lacking in resources may not have the leadership personnel to accomplish blitz remediation.
- Increased tension and lowered morale in the department that is being remediated.
- Feelings of resentment among employees.
- Intensive remediation means disruption of service and scheduling. Leaders often will have to be available to work at all hours.

The point of remediation is not punitive but restorative. The increased leadership presence is not meant to catch people doing things wrong; rather, it is to find teachable moments to coach and improve performance, and that is exactly how it must be framed for the employees. The best way to begin that process is for the leadership team to meet, strategize and determine the critical issues that must be addressed, as well as what objectives must be accomplished and everyone's role in the process. Often, a SWOT analysis (Strengths, Weaknesses, Opportunities and Threats) can prove helpful in developing such a plan.

The term "remediation" implies education, and the next step is to communicate that to the employees, speaking to it in the positive by using terms and phrases like quality improvement and investment through education.

The objectives of blitz remediation are to:

1) Evaluate each and every individual's skill according to the expected standard.

2) Identify each individual's strengths and limitations.

3) Counsel the individual to set collaborative goals in order to:

   a) Make their strengths stronger.
   b) Raise their performance in the areas of limitation so that it meets a minimum standard.

4) Provide opportunities for coaching and practice.

5) Evaluate their skills, again according to expected standards, to assess improvements.

6) Provide feedback in coaching sessions.

Upper management and/or corporate support are also critical. The leadership team must keep itself accountable and create systems of checks and balances, as well as regularly meet to review progress and problem solve challenges that emerge. Following this process, the leadership team can meet and review each individual employee's performance.

There are four possible outcomes of mass remediation:

Outcome	Follow up & Plan of Action
1) Individual fully to standard	Continue to mentor and provide further opportunities for growth
2) Individual mostly to standard, with some areas requiring improvement	Build on strengths and continue to coach to help the individual reach the expected standard
3) Individual, in most areas, requires improvement and some areas is up to standard	Requires more intensive performance management and regular ongoing monitoring and evaluation
4) Individual completely substandard	Move to termination

Case Study Organization B: Blitz Remediation

Like organization A, organization B had typical features of entitlement culture. However, upon first glance everything appeared normal. In this organization, it appeared that there were few problems. The employees appeared to get along and morale seemed to be high. However, in this case the change leader slowly began to discover that, unlike organization A, which was overtly negative, organization B was covertly negative. The employees described themselves as a family; however, they were like a mafia crime family, as evidenced by:

- Bullying and alienation towards the top achievers
- Employees victimizing one another
- Threatening and intimidating messages and notes left around as an attempt to alienate and isolate certain employees
- Culture of silence
- High turnover rate—employees transferring out and refusing to do exit interviews
- Lack of teamwork
- Negative factions and cliques
- Sabotage towards the change leader
- Constant complaining
- Passive aggressive behavior
- Employees setting each other up to fail
- Taking extended breaks and leaving early
- Poor client care, including allegations of abuse from consumers
- Health and safety concerns

Unlike organization A, this group maintained that they were a high performance team. Many of its members boasted about being employed there for over 25 years. They talked as if they were progressive. However, there was no evidence of employees upgrading their education or even having a performance appraisal, in which they were expected to have achieved any type of goals, in over 10 years. The change leader in this organization was dealing with an employee culture that said all the right things but acted in the complete opposite way. Using the ACT model, the change leader began the change process.

Component 1) Integrate ACT Into You, As The Change Leader.

The change leader made it a point to be very visible among the employees. By being assertive, collaborative and transparent, he earned the trust of a very small number of top achieving employees. They began to "blow the whistle" and break the silence about the misconduct and malpractice issues that were occurring below the surface. The change leader responded by assertively calling employees out on their practice and taking them to task. He showed the ability to collaborate by taking time to coach them and he made it a point to be transparent and consistent with everyone.

Component 2) Assess Individual Employee's Achievement and Aptitude

The change leader then assessed individual employees and ascertained that only 7% of employees were Change Agents, 50% sat on the fence and a shocking 42% of the organization were negative Instigators and Burnouts.

Component 3) Assess Organizational Culture

The fact that almost half of the employees in the organization were negative Instigators and Burnouts was daunting. There were not enough Change Agents to impact serious change and most of them were afraid to speak out due to a fear of retaliation and ostracism. Numerous attempts were made by the change leader to have employee meetings to address concerns, arrange education and issue memos; however, they were met with ambivalence and resistance. He even tried to praise and reward the negative employees when they did perform well, but those efforts were ignored and the complaint that "he doesn't appreciate us" continued according to the expected template.

After a year and a half of trying, the change leader realized that he had to use drastic measures, especially because the issues of misconduct were so severe. According to his assessment, over 75% of the employees were performing below industry standards.

Components 4) & 5) Influence Employee Behavior Change Towards Culture Of Achievement /Empower, Recognize And Performance Manage

The change leader developed a plan with his superiors and peer leaders, who were very supportive and saw the urgency in this situation. Blitz remediation ensued for a two-month period. All employees had their skills formally assessed, then met with the change leader and his team to set up goals according to their strengths, limitations and interests. Education was offered regularly and employees were relieved of duties to attend. The change leader and his team increased their presence in the departments to observe and to be on hand to deal with issues that arose. Often they took opportunities not only to correct performance but also to give praise when they encountered positive performance from employees.

At the end of the two-month period, the employees were told that they would have their skills re-assessed to determine if they had met their goals. At the end of the process, employees were given a report card and feedback on their performance. The end result was that the majority of employees experienced a noticeable improvement in their overall work performance.

The table below illustrates the results. The blitz remediation occurred between years 2 and 3. The result was the majority of employees actually improved their performance. The spring of year 3 showed a positive 71% shift, compared to the negative 92% downward shift in year 1

The ACT of Change Management

Table 2: Organization B

	Spring Year 1	Spring Year 2	Spring Year 3	Summer Year 4
+ **Change Agents**	7%	24%	33%	40%
+/− **Status Quo**	50%	40%	38%	40%
− **Instigators/ Burnouts**	42%	36%	29%	20%

Graph 2: Organization B

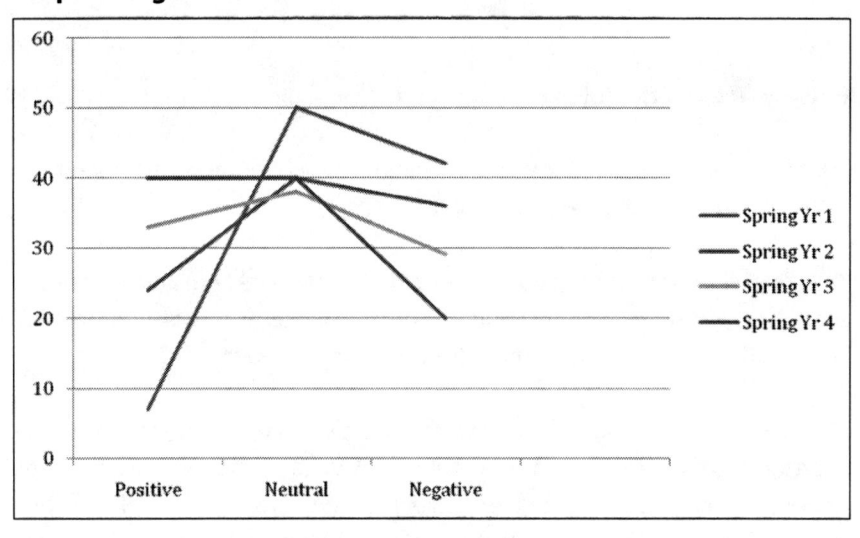

Spring Years 1 and 2 illustrate a negative skew, indicating entitlement culture.

Spring Year 3 shows an almost level line, indicating a transition that occurred after an intense process of remediation, which became the tipping point.

Due to the passive aggressive culture of Organization B, the process of change took longer and required more resources, as well as a more intensive approach. However Organization B successfully moved from a culture of entitlement to a culture of achievement, as evidenced by:

- Increased recruiting

- Increased number of employees taking educational opportunities

- Decreased client complaints

- The termination of a few extremely negative employees

- Overall improved morale evidenced by decreased tension and more collegiality in the workplace

- The majority of employees working up to industry standards

Review Of Key Principles

The ability to see opportunity in crisis and turn disadvantage into advantage is the mark of an effective change leader.

At times when it is not feasible to empower Change Agents and there are serious concerns regarding conduct, performance and safety, then blitz remediation is an effective option for the change leader.

The point of remediation is actually not punitive but restorative. The increased leadership presence is meant not to catch people doing things wrong; rather, it is to find teachable moments to coach and improve performance, and that is exactly how it must be framed to the employees.

CHAPTER 10

Conclusion & Review of Key Principles

Whatever Became Of Nathan?

In the introduction of this book, we met Nathan, a new aspiring change leader who had just entered his organization only to find that he had a monumental task ahead of him. Like Nathan, few are prepared for what challenges and obstacles await them in the change journey. This book was written with the Nathan's of the world in mind, and for any new change leader; it was meant to clearly lay out the reality of change management, including the personal and professional sacrifices that often come with the process. I am glad to report that Nathan was successful in his change journey. However it wasn't all about Nathan. It was also about his superiors, who were supportive of him, creating an environment in which he could flourish and grow. They allowed him to rise and fall, but they were there to coach and help him find his way. Nathan also experienced the success of the people below him, who he managed. Many of his employee experienced growth under his leadership. The organization also experienced operational success due to his implementing positive change.

Our journey through the ACT of Change Management began with the depressing reality of what is truly involved in making positive change.

Budgetary shortfalls	Excessive meetings
Excessive work hours	Fear
Excessive workload	Anxiety/Depression
Increased union grievances	Stress
Employee resistance	Sleep deprivation
Time management pressures	Self-doubt
Excessive paperwork	

I started the book with a warning to illustrate the realities of change management, which we rarely hear from the motivational speaker or leadership author. However, I also promised that I would end on a positive note by giving you the benefits of the change journey.

WARNING

The change leader and those positively impacted by the change management process, will likely experience the following:

<u>Greater Job Satisfaction</u>

Arguably, there is no greater feeing than being an instrumental part in resurrecting an organization and contributing to its turnaround.

<u>Sense Of Empowerment</u>

Leaders grow more leaders. A bonus of the change journey is the new leaders who emerge through the process. The thrill is even greater when they are revealed to be the people whom you least expected to take the lead.

<u>Increased Morale</u>

To see employees happy, empowered and productive far outweighs any personal gain for the change leader. To actually look forward to coming to work is a reward in itself.

Better Organizational Reputation In The Community

Clients and consumers seek out positive organizations and if they are treated well, word of mouth travels fast and opens new doors of opportunity.

Creativity

Sometimes the most bizarre, crazy and spontaneous idea is the one that actually works. Give yourself and others permission to think outside the box.

Budgetary Savings

Higher morale means lower absenteeism, fewer labor management costs and greater operational efficiency.

Character Development

You don't know what you are made of until you are tested. As we have seen, this process will tell you who you are as a leader.

Strengthened Bonds Between Employee And Leader

When your employees start looking out for you, then you know you have made it.

More Team Work

Together, everyone achieves more

Better Recruitment

Good reputation makes your organization a choice employer for the next generation of leaders.

Retention

Good and loyal employees staying for the right reasons because you made the environment a safe place to grow and prosper.

Support: Above, Beside & Below

A change leader is only as effective as the people around them and positive change, to be sustained, must start from the ground up. Critical to the front line change leader's success is the people above them (senior level administration), those beside them (peers) and those below (subordinates).

The importance of all three being in harmony cannot be overstated. Senior Administration must create a positive direction for the organization and create an environment for the change leader to succeed. Peers must also come alongside and share the burden of change, as well as learn from each other's successes and failures. Subordinates must accept the change leader and buy into their vision. If any of the three are not in harmony, then imbalance occurs and positive change becomes very difficult to achieve.

>A change leader without senior administration support will grow frustrated.

>A change leader without peer support will feel isolated.

>A change leader without subordinate support will be defeated.

The change management literature says it takes years to successfully change an organization. However, even if the end result is not what the change leader had originally envisioned, small successes are still victories and the change leader will experience professional growth just by attempting the process.

When we began the change journey we identified three types of change leaders:

1) <u>The Leader Who Is Thinking About Embarking On A Journey Of Change</u>

    It is my hope that this book has provided some ideas and inspiration to help you get started, to weigh the risks and benefits as well as to begin to strategize using the tools and concepts outlined in the book.

2) <u>The Leader Who Is In The Midst Of Change And Having Difficulty</u>

    My hope is that this book will serve as an aid in making a course correction on the journey of change. There might be strategies that can prove helpful and perhaps some ideas that might promote reflection on what is not working and how to turn things around.

3) <u>The Leader Who Has Experienced Success In Promoting Positive Change In Their Organization</u>

    I commend you and hope that the concepts in this book will serve as validation for a job well done.

Regardless of which category you fit, I hope the journey through the ACT of Change Management has left you more excited and energized about the benefits that can come from promoting positive change in your organization.

Review Of Key Principles

Few who read books do so in one sitting. Often people read chapters gradually as they come and go and sometimes with long intervals in between. Concepts often get lost at these times, so for the sake of reference all the key points from each chapter have been summarized below.

Chapter One: Vision & Change Dynamics

Vision is what distinguishes great leaders.

During the change process, the person who changes most is the change leader.

Deming's Law states 80% of problems in an organization are caused by systems and process and 20% by people.

The more control employees have over their environment, the higher their level of job satisfaction.

Sometimes the most profound change happens when there is scarcity or a lack of resources.

Change leaders need to be prepared for the fact that employees can fall anywhere on the continuum of change, and must plan accordingly.

People have to allow themselves to be made uncomfortable in order to be challenged and to grow.

Chapter Two: Change Theory & ACT

Other change models are based on the change leader doing things differently. The ACT model of change management presents another view of change management, which entails the change leader *being the change* and not just doing change.

In order to be successful as a change leader, he or she must be introspective and able to look within in order to examine their own character. They must also be authentic.

Before people will accept a change process, they must first accept the change leader.

The change leader must also be very relationship focused and make attempts to connect with their employees on an everyday basis. They must also actively sell their vision through everyday opportunities and interactions. This also applies to the most negative resistors.

The temptation of the change leader is to avoid the negative resistor, but an effective change leader is aware that engagement at close proximity can be used to disarm even the most toxic of employees.

The goal is not to be a perfect leader but to be a balanced leader.

Chapter Three: Integrating ACT Into You

Before the change leader tries to change others he or she must first integrate ACT into themselves, both personally and professionally.

Assertiveness involves three parts: assertive language, assertive body language and assertiveness in situations.

Collaboration involves the change leader working alongside their employees and demonstrating solidarity.

Transparency means the change leader must anticipate and be aware of factors such as fundamental attribution bias when it comes to how the employees perceive the behavior of the change leader.

Adversity works to refine leadership skills and to define a change leader.

The change leader must assess where their employees fall on the change continuum and use ACT to help them respond appropriately in order to advance their vision.

Chapter Four: Employee Achievement & Aptitude

To have an effective organization, the change leader must assess employee aptitude and achievement and influence those measures using a 3-pronged strategy:

1. <u>Recognize The Status Quo</u> (covered in more detail in chapter 6)

These individuals hold up the organization; if we neglect them things fall apart. These individuals typically sit on the fence. They are the key group that needs to be positively influenced and persuaded.

2. <u>Empower The Change Agents</u> (covered in more detail in chapter 7)

These individuals are catalysts for change. They are natural leaders and are critical to the success of any change initiative.

3. <u>Performance Manage The Instigators and Burnouts</u> (covered in more detail in chapter 9)

Left unchecked, these individuals do tremendous damage. The change leader must identify them and begin the process of holding them accountable and forcing them to make a choice.

Chapter Five: Assess Organizational Culture & Behavior Change

Workplace culture:

- Represents the common beliefs, values and meaning shared by the employees in that particular setting
- It is usually understood but rarely spoken about openly by the employees
- It is pervasive and has a powerful influence on the behavior of the employees
- It will help the change leader know how to motivate the employees
- How the change leader responds to the culture will often predict their success or failure in promoting positive change.

Strategic recruiting is an important part of preventing problem employees down the road.

Changing the culture involves risk for the change leader to shake up the culture and upset the accepted order.

Adherence to standards allows the change leader to bridge the gap between an Entitlement Culture to an Achievement Culture.

A new definition of leadership: being willing to stand on your principles and then accepting the consequences for taking that stand.

Persuasion to change involves the change leader reaching the employees at an emotional level.

The more contagious the vision and message the more likely it will spread and stick with the employees.

Change sometimes happens dramatically instead of gradually.

Small changes often make a larger difference down the road.

Chapter Six: The ACT Of Empowerment

Working under a negative leader can be advantageous as it can teach us how "not to empower people."

A non traditional hierarchy is the organizational model that best supports empowerment.

A leader who truly believes in empowerment is willing to work him or her out of a job.

Selfless leaders focus on building others up versus pursuing their own ambitions.

Selfless leaders allow the people above, beside and below them to make them better.

Effective leaders are aware of their blind spot and develop ways to compensate for it.

Multiple source feedback is an effective way to determine one's blind spot.

The coaching relationship between change leader and employee shares similar values to the therapeutic relationship in healthcare between practitioner and patient.

The coaching relationship is a parallel process.

10 Principles of effective coaching include:

1. Spotting potential
2. Investing time
3. Providing ongoing feedback
4. Role modeling
5. Being real
6. Allowing for setbacks and adjusting the plan
7. Giving public recognition
8. Avoiding being too prescriptive
9. Opening doors of opportunity
10. Letting them make you better

Chapter Seven: The ACT Of Recognition

Ultimately every change leader should make their goal to persuade Status Quo employees to become Change Agents by finding their undiscovered potential and developing their talents/abilities.

Recognition = Retention.

Herzberg's Motivational Theory states that recognition is a motivating factor for job satisfaction.

Adams Equity Theory states that employees become de-motivated and experience poor job satisfaction when they feel their efforts are unrewarded.

Performance appraisal is an opportunity for investment.

Use the hamburger method in giving feedback.

Change leaders need to master the skill of negotiating needs versus wants towards reframing a problem and creating options.

Change leaders must give both formal and informal recognition.

Change leaders must ultimately win over the 60% Status Quo group by focusing on recognition.

Chapter Eight: The ACT Of Performance Management

Negative employees consist of people like Burnouts and Instigators.

In most organizations, 17% of employees are actively disengaged and working against the employer.

A change leader must force negative employees to engage in self-reflection and decision-making.

Negative employees can serve a positive purpose, as demonstrated by the Problem Employee Profile, which is used to identify organizational gaps.

Negative employees can also serve a positive purpose by acting as a barometer for the organization and change leader.

Change leaders must be prepared to declare war on negative and destructive behaviors.

Negative employees and their minions can be understood using psychological concepts such as The Stockholm Syndrome, victim mentality, mob mentality, contagion theory and psychodynamic ego defense mechanisms.

The principles of Sun Tzu can prove useful in guiding a change leader towards holding negative employees accountable for their conduct and behavior.

Performance management is designed to be restorative in nature.

Principles of Solutions Focused Brief Therapy can be helpful in coaching negative employees who are able to engage in self-reflection and are willing to take ownership of their behavior.

Some negative employees can be neutralized without active performance management.

A change leader is not responsible for the decisions made by employees, but they are responsible for the environment in which the employees make decisions.

Termination should be the last resort; this should occur when employees have basically fired themselves.

The burden of proof for termination falls on the change leader, so documentation is critical.

Even though a change leader may follow the process of performance management precisely, that may not guarantee a termination in some extreme cases.

Chapter Nine: Making The Case For ACT

The ability to see opportunity in crisis and turn disadvantage into advantage is the mark of an effective change leader.

At times when it is not feasible to empower Change Agents and there are serious concerns regarding conduct, performance and safety, then blitz remediation is an effective option for the change leader.

The point of remediation is actually not punitive but restorative. The increased leadership presence is meant not to catch people doing things wrong; rather, it is to find teachable moments to coach and improve performance, and that is exactly how it must be framed to the employees.

Chapter Ten: Conclusion

Positive change in an organization can result in the following:

- Greater job satisfaction
- Sense of empowerment
- Increased morale
- Better organizational reputation in the community
- Creativity
- Budgetary savings
- Character development
- Strengthened bonds between employee and leader
- More team work
- Better recruitment and retention

BIBLIOGRAPHY

Adams, J.S. "Inequity in social exchange." (1965). *Adv. Exp. Soc. Psychol.* 62: 335-343.

Bennis, Warren G. and Robert J. Thomas. (2002). "Crucibles of leadership." *Harvard Business Review,* Sep.: 2-8

Bruce, Anne. (2003). *Building a high morale workplace.* New York: Mc Graw Hill.

Cava, Roberta. (1999) *Dealing with difficult people.* Toronto: Key Porter Books Limited.

Citrin, James M. and Smith, Richard A. (2003*). The 5 patterns of extraordinary careers: The guide for achieving success and satisfaction.* New York: Crown Business Books/Esaress Holding , Ltd. Gallup Poll. *Gallup Management Journal. 2009.*

George, Bill et al. "Discovering your authentic leadership." *Harvard Business Review.* Feb 2007: 1-8

Gladwell, Malcolm. (2002). *The Tipping point: How little things can make a big difference.* New York:L Chapter 9 will present case studies that will provide tangible examples of the ways in which this strategy can be used to spur successful organizational change. ittle, Brown and Company.

Gorden, Raymond L. (1992). *Basic interviewing skills.* Long Grove Illinois: Waveland Press Inc.

Guiness, Os. (2005). *Unspeakable: Facing up to the challenge of evil.* New York, NY: Harper Collins.

Herzberg, F., Mausner, B. & Snyderman B.B. (1959). *The motivation to work.* New York, NY: John Wiley.

Hoff, Ron. (1992) *I Can See You Naked: A New Revised Edition of National Bestseller on Making Fearless Presentations.* Kansas City, MO: Universal Press Syndicate.

I.K.Berg. (1994). *Family based services: A solution-focused approach.* New York: Norton.

Imundo, Louis V. (1991). *The effective supervisor's handbook, 2nd ed.* New York: AMACOM.

Johns, Gary. (1988). *Organizational behavior: Understanding life at work.* Montreal: Harper Collins.

Johnson, Meagan and Larry Johnson. (2010). *Generations, Inc.: From boomers to linksters—managing the friction between generations at work.* New York: Amacom.

Koch, Richard. (1998) *The 80/20 principle: The secret to success by achieving more with less.* New York: Random House.

Kotter, John P and Dan S. Cohen. (2002). *The heart of change: Real life stories of how people change their organizations.* Boston: Harvard Business School Press.

Kouzes. Jim and Barry Posner. (2007). *The leadership challenge 4th ed.* San Francisco: Jossey Bass.

Kübler-Ross, E. (1969). *On death and dying.* New York: Routledge.

Lencioni, Patrick. (2002). *The five dysfunctions of a team: A leadership fable.* San Francisco: Jossey Bass.

Luft, Joseph and Ingham, Harry. (1995). *The Johari window, a graphic model of interpersonal awareness:*

Proceedings of the western training laboratory in-group development. Los Angeles: UCLA.

Miller, Laurence. (2008). *From Difficult to disturbed: Understanding and managing dysfunctional employees.* New York, NY: AMACOM.

Mansfield, Stephen. (2004). *The character and greatness of Winston Churchill: Hero in a time of crisis.* Nashville: Cumberland House Publishing Inc.

Maxwell, John. (1995). *Developing the leaders around you.* Nashville: Thomas Nelson Publishers.

Maxwell, John. (2001). *The 17 indisputable laws of teamwork.* Nashville: Thomas Nelson Publishers.

Pincus, Marilyn. (2004). *Managing difficult people: A survival guide for handling any employee.* Avon. Massachusetts: FW Publications.

Rohm, Robert A. (1997). *Who do you think you are anyway? How your unique personality style acts, interacts and reacts with others.* Atlanta: Personality Insights.

Ryan, D. & Marlowe, B. (2004) "Build-a-case: A brand new CME technique that is peculiarly familiar." *Journal of Continuing Education in the Health Professions,* (24), 112-118

Sperry, Len. (1996). *Corporate therapy and consulting.* New York: Brunnel/Mazel, Inc.

Tao, General Hanzang, translated by Yuan Shibing. (2000). *Sun Tzu's Art of War: A Modern Chinese Interpretation.* New York. Sterling Publishing Company Inc.

Thomas-Kilmann Conflict Mode Instrument (also known as the TKI). Mountain View, CA: CPP, Inc, 1974-2009.

Tuckman, B.W. and Jenson, M.A. (1977). "Stages of small group development revisited." *Group & Organizational Studies,* 2. 419-42.

Watkins, Michael. (2003). *The first 90 days: Critical success strategies for new leaders at all levels*. Boston: Harvard Business School Press.

Zacharias, Ravi. (2007). *Beyond Opinion: Living The Faith We Defend*. Nashville: Thomas Nelson Publishers.

INDEX

A

Achievement Culture 81
ACT Expanded Beyond the Workplace 48
ACT Model Illustration 19, 157
Adversity 48
Appreciative Inquiry 25
Argument Perspective 125
Assertiveness 37
Assessing Aptitude & Achievement 64
Authentic Leader 27

B

Blind Spot 98
Blitz Remediation: Mass Performance Management 163
Bridging the Gap 83
Burnouts 62

C

Change Agents 58
Change Continuum 52
Change Leader Role 12
Change Unpopular Concept 12
Changing Mindset 73

Check-ins 30
Collaboration 43
Critical Mass 23
Coaching Relationship 104
Coaching Relationship Self Assessment 105
Coaching, Parallel Process 108
Coaching, Ten Principles of Effective 110
Conflict Style 124
Culture, Shake up 83
Culture, Workplace 78

D

Dis-empowerment 93
Declaration of War 143

E

Entitlement Culture 81
Equity Theory, Adams 118

F

Family vs. Team 82
Feedback, Hamburger Method 120
Financial Investment Principles 129
Fundamental Attribution Bias 47

G

Gladwell, Malcolm 23

Graphing Analysis 66

H

Hierarchical Structure 96

High Risk High Reward 81

Homework 123

Hypersight 2

I

Ideal Picture 6

Instigator 61

Integrity 36

Introspective Leader 27

J

Johari Window 100

K

Kotter, John 22

Kouzes Jim & Barry Posner 23

L

Living the Change 4

Loss & Discomfort 15

M

Momentum 15

Motivation-Hygiene Theory, Herzberg's 118

Multiple Source Feedback 102

N

Negative Employee Barometer 142

Negotiation Theory 124

P

Pareto Principle 21

Performance Appraisal 119

Performance Management, Principles and Goals of 150

Persuasion to Change 87

Positive Psychology 25

Principles & Values 3

Problem Employee Profile 139

Problem Employees Useful? 141

Proximity 32

Psychopathology of Negative Employee 145

R

Recognition, Formal & Informal 131

Recognition & Retention 117

Reflective Practice 44, 136

Reframing 121

Resources, Lack of 14

S

Selfless Leadership 97

Separating Issues 123

Status Quo 59

Strategic Recruiting 79

Sun Tzu 147

Support: Above, Beside and Below 174

T

Teachable Moments 28

Team Development Theory 24

Templates 132

Thinking Big Working Small 4

Time out 123

"Tipping" Towards Change 23

Traditional Thinking 72

Transcendence 49

Transparency 45

Tuckman, Bruce W. 24

W

Where to Focus Change 9

Why Change at All? 11

Workplace Culture Assessment 75

Worksheet #1 64

Worksheet #2 65

ABOUT THE AUTHOR

Steve holds an undergraduate degree in psychology and is graduate trained in cognitive behavioral therapy. He also holds certification as an ombudsman and is experienced in negotiation theory and alternative dispute resolution. Steve is also a certified human behavior consultant specializing in personality dimensions which he regularly integrates into many of his seminars and workshops.

For over 15 years Steve Mathew has trained all ranges of professionals across Canada and parts of the U.S. on topics related to clinical care, leadership and organizational dynamics. Steve has held several leadership positions throughout his career most notably as a clinical manager in a hospital setting.

Additionally, Steve is a co owner of MDM Consulting. Through his training and consulting practice he has assisted several organizations achieve positive change in both culture and service delivery. Steve has authored several publications including magazine articles in healthcare trade journals and co-authored the *book "Breaking Through: Working with the Frail Elderly."*

Steve and his family reside in the Greater Toronto Area. They pride themselves as a family of the outdoors spending their summers camping and canoeing throughout Ontario.